BREAKING THROUGH BARRIERS TO

BLESSING

OVERCOMING SINS, WOUNDS AND DEMONS

DAVID LEGGE

malcolm down
PUBLISHING

British Library Cataloguing in Publication Data
A catalogue record for this book is available from the British Library.
ISBN 978-1-910786-71-0
All Scripture quotations, unless otherwise indicated, are taken from
The Holy Bible, New King James Version, Copyright 1982 by Thomas
Nelson Inc.

Scripture quotations marked 'The Message' are taken from The
Message. Copyright 1993, 1994, 1995, 1996, 2000, 2001, 2002. Used by
permission of NavPress Publishing Group.

Cover design by Esther Kotecha
Art direction by Sarah Grace
Printed in the UK by Bell & Bain Ltd, Glasgow

DEDICATION

I dedicate this book to my precious wife, Barbara.
You are a gift from God to me. Thank you for all your love,
support and encouragement in life and ministry.

ACKNOWLEDGEMENTS

Thank you to my dear friend and webmaster of *preachtheword.com*, Andrew Watkins, for all your help in preparation for this publication. Also, many thanks to those anonymous proof readers who helped so willingly.

WHAT OTHERS ARE SAYING...

———•———

In this broken world with its many conflicts, many are asking the question, *Where is God in all of this?* David offers us practical help in this book, which encourages us to get back to the infallible Word of God – the divine manual for victorious living. David reminds us of the root of all barriers to blessing, and invites us not only to read the Scriptures, but apply them in our daily living – so that we can experience breaking through barriers to *real* blessing. Let us also remember that we are all a work in progress as we are transformed into the likeness of Christ. Through this book, God will inspire and lead you to experience your freedom in Christ and be an overcomer.

David L'Herroux
United Christian Broadcasters (UCB) Chief Executive

In my father's day, the usual areas of bondage were smoking, drinking and swearing. Today our culture is awash with additional areas of darkness: pornography, drugs, the occult, sexual immorality, abortion, violence, rebellion against authority, fatherlessness, self-harm, anxiety, fear and youth suicide. As God graciously adds to the number of those being saved, such areas of bondage are coming to the fore within church congregations and many leaders feel ill-equipped to deal with them.

There are books available which deal with particular areas of bondage in great depth, but this book does something different, and does it well. It skilfully skims a stone over all these waters, giving enough information to confirm the reality of these bondages, but just as importantly, the biblical mandate for this ministry.

It also does much to explain the spiritual realm, especially the role of the demonic in the unseen realm, in such a clear, biblical and logical way that it not only removes fear of this much-ignored subject, but hopefully generates a desire to learn more.

It is my prayer that this book will become essential reading, not just for church leaders, ministry teams and lay people, but as recommended reading in Bible Colleges and Seminaries. It is biblical, accurate, well-written, and greatly needed for such a time as this!

Ken Symington
Founder of Christian Restoration in Ireland; international
Christian speaker; author of *Loved Like Never Before* and *The Great Adventure – the challenge of really following Jesus.*

This book is a real gem of an explanation of the healing and deliverance ministry of Jesus. David has skilfully drawn together, along with his own very helpful insights, the teaching of many who have been seeking to understand this ministry over recent years.

He has clearly addressed the rightful balance necessary when praying for those needing help with both inner wounding and inner bondage. David's book is remarkably thorough, pleasingly uncomplicated, truly practical and very well founded in Scripture.

The restoration journey for a follower of Jesus will inevitably encounter the hurdles of sins, wounds and demons. Understanding how each of these is to be tackled, in accordance with the Bible, is such an important issue for the effectiveness of the Body of Christ in these days.

David Cross
Deputy International Director
Ellel Ministries

In a day and age when modern medicine is being seriously challenged in finding thorough cures for debilitating illnesses, David Legge takes us into a deep and insightful understanding of the roots and causes of problems that so often challenge people in both their spiritual and physical lives. David offers a biblical and carefully researched look into how we can attain sustainable breakthroughs amidst the many challenges people are experiencing today. He probes such issues as 'fear' and how this can be addressed through the power of prayer, based on appropriating the promises of the cross. I thoroughly recommend this book since it draws on the promises of Scripture, gives in-depth insight into many of the biblical miracles and healings, and provides answers to many questions in a practical and tangible way, that will lead to breakthrough and blessing!

Rev. Dr. Alistair P. Petrie
Executive Director
Partnership Ministries
www.partnershipministries.org

This is a book that stops us in our tracks and causes us to rethink our position as Christians. The key emphasis is on *being* rather than *doing*. As we enter into a living, vital relationship with God we are empowered to live a life of fellowship and communion with God. A life that is pleasing to God and enriching for us. Here the author outlines the steps of forgiveness, freedom and wholeness. This is a balanced book giving us an insight into the demonic world, its influences and snares, at the same time guarding us against being overwhelmed by it and pointing us to the One who came to 'set the captives free'. For many who are struggling with life's issues and mysteries, here is a book that will help them discover a new life of freedom in the healing, delivering ministry of the Lord Jesus Christ. I strongly recommend it.

Rev. T.J. Hagan B.D.
Minister Emeritus, Donacloney Presbyterian Church, Lurgan,
Northern Ireland

CONTENTS

INTRODUCTION

—•—

'Why me?' must be somewhere near to number one in the top ten of the most commonly asked questions in life. Another question, *'Why not me?'* is often asked by Christians who feel that God's blessings are eluding them. Their lives do not correspond to either famous biblical characters or their historic spiritual heroes. They even look at some of their contemporaries with envy, because their own spiritual life seems to fall far short in comparison. There appear to be some barriers to blessing; obstacles to maturing as a Christian. It is as if there is a blockage in the way, obstructing what they know to be God's declared will for their lives. Something like an invisible and malevolent force field is somehow wedged between them and God, preventing intimacy with Him. Does this describe your experience?

Many Christians, if they are honest, feel let down or secretly even somewhat of a fraud because of the absence of blessing and victory in their lives. This complex is further compounded by the claims that are often made through some Christian teaching. Many are led to believe that when they embrace the gospel, they will be so radically changed that most, if not all, of their spiritual problems will be solved. We do not for a moment lessen the power of the cross and the resurrection of Christ, but why is the experience of so many Christians much less than what they are often led to expect?

Part of the answer to that question is surely that Christian conversion is not the end of our spiritual search and transformation, but rather the beginning. The new birth is a threshold experience that opens for us the door of salvation, but then leads us into a kind of hospital of healing in which the Great Physician, Jesus Christ, begins the process of changing us from 'glory to glory' (2 Corinthians 3:18) into His own image. So, when you become a Christian, you do not 'arrive', but rather you embark on a journey that will never end until you are like the Son of God Himself.

Has there been some undefined hindrance in your Christian life? You can't quite put your finger on it, but you know that there is something significant obstructing your progress into spiritual maturity. If that is so, this book is for you! The truth contained in these pages has already been a lifeline to many, and can set you free and pave the way to the relationship with God that you have always longed for – the one He has always intended for you.

The most common areas of hindrance – sins, wounds and demons

It is vital that the obstacles to blessings in our lives are diagnosed correctly, so that we may receive the appropriate treatment. Often the wrong condition is being addressed, or the wrong remedy is applied. This would be a good moment, before we go any further, to turn your heart towards God and ask Him to reveal to you where your real problems may lie. Why not take a moment right now, and pray something like this:

Father, in the Name of Your Son, the Lord Jesus Christ, I ask You, through the power of Your Holy Spirit, to reveal to me the barriers to blessing in my life. Thank You Father, Amen.

Sins, wounds and *demons* are the three general areas where most, if not all, problems occur.

Sins are our acts of disobedience to God's will as revealed in His Word. Whenever we disobey God through what we *do*, or what we leave *undone*, we become more vulnerable to the enemy's attacks. *Wounds* are the hurts, both internal and external, that we experience – whether self-inflicted, received at the hands of others, or obtained through a wide variety of adverse circumstances. *Demons* are actual spiritual personalities who seek, under the lordship of Satan himself, to destroy human lives. As we shall see in more detail, demons utilise our sins, the sins of others against us, and our wounds to acquire leverage in order to negatively influence our lives. Demons seek to create within us a powerbase which will drive us on in all kinds of sinful and destructive behaviours.

Of course, the solutions for each of these problem areas are different. It is crucial that the correct treatment is applied to each condition. *Sins* cannot be *healed* or *expelled*. *Wounds* cannot be *repented* of or *expelled*. *Demons* cannot be *repented* of or *healed*. *Sins* should be *repented* of, *wounds* need to be *healed*, and *demons* must be *expelled*. Why is it so important to emphasise these distinctions?

Sometimes, whenever there is strong preaching against sin (which is not necessarily wrong, of course), repentance can be emphasised to the exception of addressing personal wounds and the demonic realm. This can be why, at times, people attempt to repent, but find it almost impossible to break the cycle of sin. By no means do we wish to underestimate our own propensity to wickedness; Scripture is explicit on this. However, there are obvious cases where people desire to turn from sin, but are continually pulled back into the sequence of failure. It is well known that 'pain seeks out pleasure'. Therefore, it can be the case that our sins may have become a kind of coping mechanism for our pain. Often in such circumstances, the demonic also gets on board, bringing an empowering force to the sinful behaviour. This is why to repent is not always enough. Perhaps this might explain why you may be struggling so much with habitual sin? It may be that your sin is medicating your pain. Have you also considered how the enemy has capitalised on your hurts and disobedience, and may be driving you on in this downward spiral? This is where healing and deliverance may need to be applied.

That being said, sin must be repented of. We must own up to our personal wrongdoing and take responsibility for our actions. There may have been deep wounding in our experience, which can significantly contribute to our problems, but we cannot blame everything on hurts. Neither can we point to Satan and say, 'The devil made me do it!' Yes, as we shall see, the enemy is a formidable force indeed, but we must be real about how we have co-operated with him and submitted to his advances. Demonic influences may be cast out of people's lives, but if a person's behaviour doesn't change and wounds aren't healed, the enemy will almost certainly return.

It is not enough to preach repentance without healing and

deliverance, yet healing and deliverance must not be taught without the necessity of repentance and discipleship. There must be biblical balance.

In these pages, we will explore together how we can break through barriers to the blessing of God! We will examine in more detail *sins, wounds* and *demons* with a view to identifying and overcoming these hindrances to your progress as a Christian.

Before we proceed, may I give a word of warning? It is important that you don't become introspective and begin to apply everything in this book to yourself. Some people can be very impressionable, and the enemy can use this to overwhelm them with problems they don't actually have. Remember, Satan is the accuser of the brothers (Revelation 12:10) – he will accuse us of issues we *have* and even ones we *don't have*; whichever works best for his soul-destroying purposes! So don't allow the enemy to torment you about phantom problems. Having said that, if God's Holy Spirit witnesses with you that there could be a problem in the areas of *sins, wounds* or *demons*, you must deal with this before the Lord in order to know the liberty and life that is God's will for you in Christ Jesus.

SINS

Search me, God, and know my heart;
test me and know my anxious thoughts.
See if there is any offensive way in me,
and lead me in the way everlasting.
Psalm 139:23–24 (NIV UK 2011)

CHAPTER ONE
PERSONAL HONESTY

Repentance for sin is vital. The first command we hear from Jesus in the Gospels is:

> Repent, for the kingdom of heaven is at hand.
>
> *Matthew 4:17*

We might say that 'repent' is the first word of the gospel. Repentance should not be confused with some work of human effort in trying to make ourselves acceptable to God. The gospel is all of grace. Ephesians 2:8–9 is emphatic:

> For by grace you have been saved through faith, and that not of yourselves; it is the gift of God, not of works, lest anyone should boast.

Changing your mind

It is through faith that we receive God's free unmerited grace-gift of eternal life; but repentance is a part of that process. The most commonly used Greek word in the New Testament for 'repent' is *metanoeo* which literally means 'a change of mind'. This infers a change of mind concerning our sin, ourselves, and the person and work of Christ. It is not so much that 'repent and believe' are two separate commands, but rather two sides of the same coin. If I announce, 'I am leaving my home in County Armagh and travelling to Dublin', it sounds like there are two actions involved, when in a true sense there is only one journey taking place – because I cannot go to Dublin, or anywhere else for that matter, without leaving my home. In the same way I cannot have faith in Christ without changing the understanding of my relationship with sin and Jesus. This is repentance – the mind and the posture changes towards our sin, and towards Jesus. Of course, the Holy Spirit is the One who influences our hearts to bring us to this knowledge, which further discredits any suggestion that repentance is merely a human work of the flesh.

A common mistake that Christians make is to confine their repentance to the moment of their conversion. However, whilst that may have been their first act of repentance, it should never be the last. The 'renewing of the mind' (see Romans 12:2) is an ongoing work of the Spirit in our lives which we must continually submit to in repentant obedience as the Holy Spirit leads us into all truth.

At this point some Christians get stuck. They have not moved on in their faith journey because of a lack of ongoing repentance in response to personal revelation. Maybe they have tried to justify their sin because of the wounds they have. It could even be that there has been a very heavy influence of the evil one in their lives or family which they feel has strongly disadvantaged them. We will explore these difficult and real areas in the following pages but, before we do, a very important foundation principle must be laid down: OUR SIN MUST BE REPENTED OF.

Whatever other accentuating factors there might be, we must all take responsibility for our ungodly behaviour. Yes, our pain and the devil can make sin very hard to resist at times, even almost impossible, but we must admit that *we* are involved in the choice to sin. I want you to consider the question: 'How do I co-operate with the enemy's agenda?' What is the part that you have to play in the spiritual difficulties you are experiencing? Apart from anything else, will you be responsible for your own actions?

In ministry, needy people can come for help at times, especially prayer, but with some individuals, before long it is discernible that they wish to have a kind of 'quick fix'. It is as if they want God to 'zap 'em!' so they can go on their own merry way and enjoy life again. Of course, Jesus has come to give us life in abundance and it is Satan who comes to steal, kill and destroy (see John 10:10) – but Jesus does not give us our lives back just for us to destroy them further with sin or squander them on selfishness. At times people want to receive prayer in order to get their problems solved, but they don't want to take responsibility for their own behaviour.

No 'quick fixes' – Simon Magus

In Acts 8 we read of Simon the Magician (Magus), who appeared to have believed the gospel during a spiritual awakening in Samaria where Philip performed miracles, healings and deliverances to the astonishment of all the people. Simon had a reputation in his community for demonstrating amazing spiritual power in the occult realm. Luke records that Simon believed, was baptised and even accompanied Philip in his ministry (verse 13). The apostles in Jerusalem heard about this move of God and sent Peter and John to the region. They quickly discovered that, as yet, these believers had not received the Holy Spirit as God intended. To remedy this, Peter and John laid hands on these Christians and the Holy Spirit fell upon them. When Simon witnessed this incredible spiritual power, which seemed to be transferred through the apostles' touch, he was envious. He desired this 'ability' so much that he offered the apostles money so that he might have it. He said:

> Give me this power also, that anyone on whom I lay hands may receive the Holy Spirit.
>
> *Acts 8:19*

Peter's response has caused some Bible interpreters difficulty in deciding whether or not Simon actually was a genuine believer. Peter's retort to Simon was strong to say the least:

> Your money perish with you, because you thought that the gift of God could be purchased with money! You have neither part nor portion in this matter, for your heart is not right in the sight of God. Repent therefore of this your wickedness, and pray God if perhaps the thought of your heart may be forgiven you. For I see that you are poisoned by bitterness and bound by iniquity.
>
> *Acts 8:20–23*

J.B. Phillips translated verse 20:

> To hell with you and your money! How dare you think you could buy the gift of God!

Please note that Peter's immediate response to Simon was to call him to repentance and not to exorcise him of a demon. Did Simon perhaps have some demonic problems that were a kind of hangover from his past dark arts? This is possible. Peter does say Simon was '*bound* by iniquity' and '*poisoned* by bitterness'. No doubt these are classic breeding grounds for the demonic. However, Peter doesn't expel the enemy from Simon but rather commands him to repent.

Simon's answer to Peter is also very instructive in verse 24:

Pray to the Lord for me, that none of the things which you have spoken may come upon me.

Do you see what's happening here? I think the heart-cry of Simon was, in essence, 'Fix me!' He realised that what Peter said was true, but he immediately chose to look to Peter for prayer rather than taking responsibility for his actions in personal repentance.

In this age of instant gratification and technological revolution we have been conditioned to expect everything to come to us with immediate ease. With rampant individualism abroad there can also be in us a sense of entitlement, sometimes fuelled by some Christian teaching that encourages a 'gimme, gimme, gimme' attitude to God's blessings. There is no doubt that God wants to bless our socks off! He wants to bless us beyond our wildest imaginings, but the 'road less travelled' to that goal is the road of repentance.

Non-negotiable repentance

If we want to truly know God and experience the healing and freedom Jesus died for, personal repentance is vital. To neglect repentance, in the message we preach or in our personal lives, is to underestimate the devastating practical impact of sin upon our fellowship with God.

Scripture is clear:

> If I regard sin and baseness in my heart [that is, if I know it is there and do nothing about it],
> The Lord will not hear [me];
>
> *Psalm 66:18 (Amplified Bible)*

The word 'regard' in this verse could be translated 'cherish' or 'harbour'. The idea is that we can be protecting sinful ways with a deep affection. Of course, every day God hears the cries of sinners who are immersed in the deepest wickedness – this verse does not contradict that truth. Rather, the psalmist emphasises that if there is duplicity in our hearts, we have no guarantee that the Lord will hear our prayer. To put it another way: if we are reaching out to God with one hand for help, but with the other hand are holding on to a sin we love with vice-like tenacity, we are effectively undoing any potential of our prayer getting an answer.

We don't realise that God's ears are deafened to our cries when we are dishonest about the desires of our hearts. God is not looking for perfection in us, but He is looking for personal honesty. Grace and truth come together and His grace will meet us when we are truthful about our sinful hearts.

Hebrews 12:1 encourages us:

> ... let us lay aside every weight, and the sin which so easily ensnares us ...

First John 1:7 teaches us that in order to enjoy the cleansing power of the blood of Jesus we must:

... walk in the light as He is in the light ...

So, there you have it! It is the utmost presumption to expect the work of the cross to cover something that we are not prepared to uncover.

Please do not misunderstand. God expects no one to attempt to 'clean themselves up' before coming to Him. Neither does He require us to have perfect knowledge of all our failure before we approach Him. However, what He does need from us is a willingness to agree with Him concerning all our ungodly behaviour, and a willingness – with His help – to forsake it.

Some of you reading this may feel discouraged because you know the awful grip a particular sin has upon you – please don't hear what I'm not saying! I know you need a miracle to break free, and you can't do that yourself. God knows you've probably tried hundreds of times! There may well be areas of wounding that are fuelling these sinful habits and perhaps even demonic empowerment driving you on in them. Yes, it's true that repentance on its own has not been enough for many people to find freedom from their sinful behaviours – that's the reason why some of you have turned to this book, though now you may be thinking you've made a terrible mistake! Don't give up before you even start – hang in there, please! There is hope and an answer for your issues. However, that answer in Jesus and the gospel will not bypass your personal honesty and repentance. This truth is foundational to the rest of this book and, indeed, your healing and deliverance.

So, what is God asking you to do? Not fix yourself. Not run to someone else to fix you. Not incessantly pray 'gimme, gimme' prayers to Him. He is asking you to be transparent before Him and honestly answer the question: 'Am I willing to change my mind about my ungodly ways that are harming me, and others around me, and am I ready for God to take these things out of my life for good?' Even if you can't say that yet, perhaps you could pray: 'Lord, make me willing and make me ready to be honest before You about my sin.'

He who covers his sins will not prosper,
But whoever confesses and forsakes them will have mercy.

Proverbs 28:13

A Prayer

Lord Jesus, You are the Light and in You is no darkness at all. Please shine Your light into all the dark recesses of my life. Help me now to be honest with You about my sins. I want to be completely transparent before You.

I declare that You are the Son of God and the only way to God, that You died on the cross for my sins and rose again that I might be forgiven and receive eternal life.

I confess all my sins before You and hold nothing back *(please elaborate and specify particular sins)*. I repent of these sins and by faith receive Your mercy and forgiveness through Your death on the cross. Amen.

CHAPTER TWO
A STANDARD TOO HIGH

To be caught in the devastating spiral of failure after failure is a demoralising place to be. Of course, this wouldn't be as painful if you were content to be there. It is because you are frustrated with your performance that you despair. A flagrant, careless sinner never experiences the anguish of constant failure to the extent that a conscientious Christian does. In a strange way, herein lies one of our greatest problems: we can become our own worst enemy by requiring a standard too high of ourselves. Often those with a particularly religious upbringing are unaware of the extent to which this factor hinders them moving on with God. The irony, of course, is that this standard – which is too high – is born of a deep desire to please God, but actually militates against it.

The problem of perfectionism
Having read Chapter One you may conclude that I'm already

starting to contradict myself. To be so adamant that repentance and ruthlessness towards our sin is necessary, and then to suggest we beware of perfectionism, might seem counterproductive. On the contrary, this addresses the very core of the problem for many of us. Simon Magus in Acts 8 had a 'fix me' mentality towards Peter, but many of us have a 'fix me' mentality towards ourselves. Immediately we detect that there is an unwanted area of sin in our lives, we attempt to remedy it ourselves. This approach relies on the flesh and almost certainly guarantees failure. This is the age-old conflict of the weakness of the Law versus the power of the Spirit, spoken of by Paul in Romans and Galatians. Add to this the fact that there are often wounds driving us in these sinful cycles and even demonic entities empowering us. We are often predisposed to failure in any attempt to conquer our wicked behaviours.

Before we even begin to address the answer to our sin problems, we must determine to be done with perfectionism. It simply doesn't work. In fact, in a further irony, it is actually perfectionism that causes many Christians to give up in their pursuit of holiness. Let me explain. When you hold yourself to a standard too high, and you keep falling short of that standard, the most obvious decision to make is to give up completely. Most of us associate perfectionists with the high-fliers and high-achievers in life, which is a mistake. The dropout, the bum, the vagrant drifter can also be a perfectionist. How so? They have made the fatal assumption that 'If I can't do a thing perfectly I won't do it at all'. When the epiphany of their imperfection dawns upon them, the perfectionist so often will throw in the towel.

This tendency of dropping out can be seen in the lives of many Christians, not only in relation to their 'besetting' sins but in many areas of discipleship. For example, how many of us have tried a consecutive Bible reading scheme only to founder at the first or second hurdle? We start on 1 January with laudable intentions but are dispirited on 3 January when we miss our allocated daily Scripture portion. Rather than forgetting about it and taking up our reading again on 4 January, we try to catch up with the missing passages – and (perish the thought) if we miss another day, it is like an avalanche under which we get buried in remorseful failure! The easiest thing is to miss a day, then two, then a week and then the Bible reading scheme goes to the wall. What prevents us simply forgetting about the missing day and picking up again the next day? You've got it: perfectionism. This analogy could be applied in a thousand different ways to show that actually we would be more 'successful' in all our endeavours (Christian or otherwise) if we ditched perfectionist tendencies. Leanne Payne, teaching on 'The Disease of Introspection' in her Pastoral Care Ministries School, makes reference to C.S. Lewis' personal discovery that perfectionism was the reason why many potential authors never wrote the book that was inside them, because they wanted a perfect creation immediately rather than simply writing and writing until something beautiful came.[1] Would it not be better to reach 31 December having read 80 per cent of the Bible that we'd never read before, rather than the mere 2 per cent we read because we gave up in week one after sleeping in?

G.K. Chesterton was right when he stated:

If a thing is worth doing, it is worth doing badly.[2]

Of course, this is counterintuitive to those of us who have received a 'good Christian work ethic' or the like. Why wouldn't you always do your best? There is nothing wrong with trying your best, the problem comes when we won't do a thing *unless* it's the best. If a thing is worth doing, it is worth doing badly rather than not doing it at all! If it's the right thing to do, do it regardless of whether or not you do it well. So, to use our example of Bible reading again: is it not better to read some of the Bible badly than to read none at all?

If you are caught in the unbreakable sequence of consecutive failure, one of the first things you may need to do is renounce the very thing fuelling your descent: your tendency towards perfectionism. Face the irrefutable fact of our own morality: we fail. The failure rate of the human race is 100 per cent. As 'good little Christians' we may try not to fail, but inevitably we will. We are not to be easy on sin, or attempt to condone or excuse it in any way, but sometimes we just need to get over ourselves and our mistakes. If the Holy Law of God was given to us for any reason, it was to show us: YOU'RE NOT PERFECT! That's why we need a Saviour. The irony is, many people use the Law in an attempt to qualify themselves before God – the monumental mistake of all religion and many Christian believers.

The Church today, in some respects, may well be suffering because of a lowering of biblical standards, but the answer to this problem will never be creating standards for ourselves which are too high. This was the pitfall of Pharisaism and, indeed, all forms of legalism.

> They crush people with unbearable religious demands and never lift a finger to ease the burden.
>
> *Matthew 23:4 (NLT)*

In the rest of this book, there will be steps for you to take to get free from the cycle of sin, pain and the power of the enemy – but if you are caught in the perverted reasoning of perfectionism, you need to break out. What will that look like in practical terms? It looks like not giving up, and deciding that – no matter how many times you have fallen and will fall again – you will get up and pursue the answer in Jesus Christ your Lord.

> The godly may trip seven times, but they will get up again.
> But one disaster is enough to overthrow the wicked.
>
> *Proverbs 24:16 (NLT)*

Someone once said that the perseverance of the saints is made up of 10,000 new beginnings.

Introspection – the fruit of perfectionism

Introspection is the tendency to look within to examine our thoughts and feelings. The Bible encourages us in a level of self-examination but, for many, introspection has become a disease destroying the soul. The penchant to turn inward upon ourselves in a brooding self-analysis is the inevitable outworking of the perfectionist mentality. Whatever our unattainable standard might be, we use that standard to scrutinise ourselves. We are caught in the incessant compulsion of carving ourselves up on our own dissection table.

We must beware here of a clever trick of the enemy. When we become aware of our failures we look within to address them, and the enemy (who is 'the accuser of the brethren', Revelation 12:10) heaps upon us condemnation that pulls us down further and actually makes recourse to sin much easier. So, what is the alternative – ignoring the sin within? Not at all. The answer is to become present to our sin, but only in the presence of God. We are not to do the Holy Spirit's work of searching ourselves in the power of the flesh, neither are we to submit to a legalistic system or individual doing it for us. Such practices will be a gift to the enemy to condemn us to distraction. Psalm 139:23–24 answers the dilemma of how we address our sin within whilst not being introspective:

> Search me, God, and know my heart;
> test me and know my anxious thoughts.
> See if there is any offensive way in me,
> and lead me in the way everlasting.
>
> *Psalm 139:23–24 (NIV UK 2011)*

Notice the sequence of self-examination spoken of here by David. God did the internal searching of David, pointing out areas that needed his attention. David didn't become self-absorbed in destructive introversion that drove him to despair. All of us would find plenty of disturbing elements if we rummaged around inside of ourselves. There is plenty within to plunge us into depression or give Satan, the accuser, plenty of ammunition to fire back at us. This is why the biblical pattern is: ask God to show you what needs your attention and with His help address it, but don't obsess about any other frailties that the Holy Spirit is not highlighting at present. We must trust God our Father to know what we need cognisance of within, when we need to know it, and how He proposes to effectively solve it.

This tendency of turning within must be broken if we are to be set free from sin. The primary reason for this is that the answer is not within us, but outside of us: God. Of course, the Holy Spirit indwells us, but introspection is not obsession with Him but with our broken selves.

The problem of passivity

In addressing our sin, a further problem which is often overlooked is passivity. Passivity is a nonchalant acceptance of things as they are without any active response. This, of course, can be another fruit of perfectionism. We have failed so many times before and don't know how to fix it, so we give up and refuse to do anything to rectify the problem.

Even our upbringing can have a bearing upon this. If we were 'spoiled' as children or overindulged, it can foster passive tendencies. We might always be looking for someone else to solve our problems for us without lifting a finger ourselves.

The alternative is not willpower. We've already outlined the perils of relying on the flesh. Scripture also warns against 'will-worship' (see Colossians 2:23). If all we needed was willpower to solve our sin problems, we wouldn't have needed a Saviour. However, passivity will not help us. We need an active will. Many of us who have been worn down by years of defeat need our wills strengthened by God Himself – as it were, an infusing of His will into ours.

This would be a good point at which to pray for that very thing.

A Prayer

Lord Jesus, You are the Holy One and Perfection itself. I admit my own sin and sinful ways *(perhaps expand)*. I confess that at times my attempts to solve my sin problems have been deeply flawed. I renounce any false standard I have lived by. Forgive me for perfectionism, wrong introspection and passivity.

I ask that You would search me and tell me anything that I need to know about myself. Close my ears to self-deception and satanic deception, and let me hear Your voice alone.

Please strengthen my will with the Father's strong will by the power of the Holy Spirit, so that I may persevere in pursuing You to freedom. When I fall, may You give me the grace to get up again and follow You. Amen.

---

1. Recording of Leanne Payne, *The Disease of Introspection*, Wheaton Pastoral Care Ministries School, 2007.

2. G.K. Chesterton, *What's Wrong with the World* (New York: Cosimo Classics, 2007).

CHAPTER THREE
CONFESSION THAT IS GOOD FOR THE SOUL

———◦———

Confession of our sins is essentially agreeing with God that what He says about our ungodly ways is true. It is a kind of putting our hands up and admitting, 'I'm guilty as charged!' The prophet Amos spoke of God's truth as being like a plumb line by which we must measure everything. God's truth is the true standard. Of course, God's holiness is too high a standard for us to attain on our own, and so confession is when we concede that we fall short of the mark. Again, the prophet asks in Amos 3:3:

Can two walk together, unless they are agreed?

So, whilst we must be done with all perfectionism and the self-delusion that we can achieve too high a standard, we equally must acknowledge our deficiencies when compared to God's measure. Personal honesty through confession of sin is essential, because Jesus said:

You will know the truth, and the truth will set you free.

John 8:32 (NIV UK 2011)

As we have already said, grace and truth meet together. If we want to experience the free favour and unmerited forgiveness of God, we must meet Him on the ground of truth. Honesty and transparency are fundamental.

This emphasis must be made, not least because many people are seeking a Saviour from pain, but not a Saviour from sin. There is healing and deliverance in the message of Jesus Christ and the gospel, but sometimes healing and deliverance have been wrongly isolated from the process of discipleship. This may then result in needy people seeking the 'quick fix', but not submitting to Jesus as Lord of their lives and committing to truly follow Him. The tragedy is, even when they do receive an initial measure of help, it is short-lived, because they are not genuinely pursuing the Lord.

Confession that challenges strongholds of the mind

True confession not only admits our wrong deeds, but also exposes our warped thinking. Of course, our sinful actions are usually preceded by a thought or two. However, what we are highlighting here is more than merely tempting thoughts, but rather the powerful compulsion of strongholds of the mind. A mental 'stronghold' is like a castle of lies that has been built, often over many years, in the shelter of which the enemy's power can operate unchallenged. We could describe these strongholds of the mind as our ungodly mindsets, our thought patterns, or psychological processes that facilitate sin.

One cannot underestimate the power of these mental strongholds. An expression often used for our thought processes is 'the tracks of thought'. Like train tracks, they lead us to an inevitable destination. I often think of these mind tracks as being more like the tracks that a four-wheel-drive would gouge out on a muddy jungle trail. After years of traffic, those tracks, dug deep, would become the only route for the wheels of any vehicle to follow. Our thought patterns can similarly become so ingrained that we cannot conceive of ever thinking any differently. A mental stronghold is truly a bondage of the mind.

The good news is that in the gospel we can have 'renewed minds' (see Romans 12:2), to the extent that we can receive the very 'mind of Christ' (1 Corinthians 2:16). Eventually, those old mud tracks can be replaced with a new trail, which will become our default route. Whilst the trenches of that passage may be faint at first, eventually – with the help of the Spirit and the Word of God – the new trail will become well established and the old one will be obliterated through lack of use.

One of the first steps on the journey of renewing the mind is repentance (a change of mind), articulated in confession. Of course, what appears to be confession could be mere lip service. However, whenever confession is genuine, it is a most powerful thing. Confession to God essentially brings our sins up and out of us to Him. We are voluntarily revealing what we feel convicted about within. This is why confession often 'sticks in our throats'; we fear exposure. We must get to the point of desperation in order to authentically confess.

The power of confession to God

When the prophet Isaiah encountered the Lord in glory, splendour and holiness, his immediate reaction was one of conviction for his sin, and revulsion at it. The fruit of this encounter with the Holy, Holy, Holy One was confession:

Woe is me, for I am undone!
Because I am a man of unclean lips,
And I dwell in the midst of a people of unclean lips;
For my eyes have seen the King,
The LORD of hosts.

Isaiah 6:5

I wonder what specific sin of the lips the great prophet was confessing? Ironically, Isaiah has come to be known as the Shakespeare of the Old Testament text, because of his rich literary skills – yet his Achilles' heel seems to have been his words. Was he prone to exaggeration? Was he using inappropriate or vulgar language? Was he engaging in slander and criticism or, conversely, flattery? He was a prophet, so did his sin relate in some way to how he executed his gift? We'll never know, though it is interesting to consider that the prophet's strength – words – became his greatest weakness.

The power of confession is graphically evidenced by God's response to Isaiah's disclosure:

Then one of the seraphim flew to me, having in his hand a
live coal which he had taken with the tongs from the altar.
And he touched my mouth with it, and said:
'Behold, this has touched your lips;
Your iniquity is taken away,
And your sin purged.'

Isaiah 6:6–7

A blood-soaked, fire-infused coal was taken off the altar and applied to his sin. What a picture of the power of Christ's sacrifice in our lives! The power of the blood of Jesus and the fire of the Spirit of God applied to our confessed sin will make the difference. Isaiah then received, as it were, a recommissioning to the prophetic ministry (remember, he had already been operating in prophetic ministry with these 'lip' issues!).

The power of confession to one another

Obviously, the Bible encourages us to confess our sins to God, but what many overlook is the fact that it also exhorts us to confess our sins to each other:

Confess your trespasses to one another, and pray for one another, that you may be healed.

James 5:16

Many evangelicals have been made afraid of confession to one another because of some abuses of confession in certain quarters of Christendom. Neither we as individuals, nor any member of the clergy, for that matter, have the power to absolve someone's sins before God. This is not what we are talking about when referring to confession of sins to one another. It is clear that only God can forgive sins (Mark 2:7). However, there is a great power in confessing our faults to each other, which has been neglected for too long. James 5:16 indicates that actual healing might even flow as a consequence of such confession.

Let me explain why confession to another is so important. When Adam and Eve fell into sin at the beginning, their first instinct was to hide from God. Genesis tells us it was fear that caused them to hide (Genesis 3:10). We do the same today. When we sin, we feel so ashamed at how we've let God and others down that we reason falsely, 'Why would God want to have anything to do with someone like me?' We then withdraw from relationship with our Father, which is the one relationship that we need to solve our problems. Remember, the answer we need is outside of us. Grace must come from without, but in the very moment of our deepest need we build a wall around ourselves (usually with bricks of guilt and shame), and we shut God out. This is a crucial point: because of Jesus and His death on the cross, our sin no longer needs to keep us from coming to God; but often it is our pride that builds a wall of guilt and shame around us, which prevents us getting the help we need from our heavenly Father.

In the moments after we commit sin, not only do we withdraw from relationship with God, but we also tend to withdraw from relationship with each other. Through guilt and shame (energised by pride), we disengage from those in the Body of Christ who can minister His life to us. In our struggles with sin, we must not be isolated from deep relationships. There is healing for us there – in relationship with God and with one another. Obviously, we must have confidence in those in whom we confide. Beware of opening your heart carelessly to anyone. However, we must find true community and friendships in which we can be completely candid about how things are with us. A critical element of true relationship with God and others is that we bring everything – especially our struggles, doubts, quarrels and temptations – into relationship. Rather than running away from God and others when we sin, we should resist the fearful instinct to hide, and we should run into Father's arms and to those on earth who best exhibit His love and life.

Does this sound nonsensical to you, this talk of 'bringing your sin into relationship with God'? Well, if we are not talking to God about our sin struggles, clearly we must be hiding them from Him. Hiding from Him, and hiding from those who minister Him to us, will get us nowhere.

Why not try engaging in an explicit disclosure of your struggles to God right now? Confess your sins to Him honestly. Maybe even find a person you can really trust, and share your burden with them.

This is the message which we have heard from Him and declare to you, that God is light and in Him is no darkness at all. If we say that we have fellowship with Him, and walk in darkness, we lie and do not practice the truth. But if we walk in the light as He is in the light, we have fellowship with one another, and the blood of Jesus Christ His Son cleanses us from all sin.

If we say that we have no sin, we deceive ourselves, and the truth is not in us. If we confess our sins, He is faithful and just to forgive us our sins and to cleanse us from all unrighteousness.

1 John 1:5–9

Bear one another's burdens, and so fulfil the law of Christ.

Galatians 6:2

A Prayer

Lord Jesus, I declare that You are the Truth and everyone who is of the truth hears Your voice.

Forgive me for when I have hidden myself from You out of fear. Forgive me for the times I have withdrawn from relationship with You and others because I dreaded rejection. Please reveal to me Your love which drives out all fear. I admit that sometimes pride has produced false guilt and shame in me, which the enemy has used to hinder me approaching You. I renounce all pride and any dignity that does not come from You. I humble myself before You and come to You in my need. I freely confess all my sins and hold nothing back *(be specific if you can)*. I repent of these sins. I also confess and renounce the strongholds of my mind where the lies of the enemy reside *(if you can identify those lies, do so now)*.

I choose to agree with Your truth and I ask the Holy Spirit to renew my mind to think like You, Lord.

Finally, Lord, I ask You to bring me into the fellowship of those whom I can trust, that I might share my burdens with them, and find healing in confession. Amen.

CHAPTER FOUR
IS HOLINESS EVEN POSSIBLE?

Is holiness possible? Well, it depends upon what you mean by holiness. When you say 'holiness', many people hear 'perfection'; but holiness and perfection are not the same thing. Human perfection is not possible in this life, but holiness is. Right away, we have another reason why perfectionism is a foolish use of our energies!

Lethal legalism

Legalism – the belief that we can earn God's favour by keeping some kind of code (whether derived from the Bible, some other sacred writ, or of our own making) – breeds perfectionism, and consequently defeat, because it is impossible to achieve. Yet this is the type of pseudo-holiness that many Christians aspire to – *'stop doing bad stuff and start doing good stuff'*. This is at the heart of the phenomenon of man-made religion. On a surface level, this may appear laudable, but the tragic irony is that it is this very falsehood that keeps many locked into a seemingly unbreakable failure cycle.

Neil Anderson, Rich Miller and Paul Travis, in their wonderful book *Breaking the Bondage of Legalism*[1], cite a 2002 George Barna Research Group poll which they commissioned in preparation for the writing of their book. The survey was taken among Christians nationwide in the USA, to discover how widespread legalism was in the American Church. One of the six survey statements was:

The Christian life is well summed-up as 'trying to do what God commands'. How would you respond to that statement?

If you agree with that statement as a good summary of the Christian life, you would be in the majority of 57 per cent who 'strongly agreed'. A further 25 per cent 'somewhat agreed', which gave a total of 82 per cent in agreement with this synopsis of Christianity. However, as Anderson, Miller and Travis point out, the only problem with this summary of the Christian life is: IT'S WRONG!

Many professing Christians operate within a performance-based relationship with God. Their expression of faith is characterised more by keeping rules than abiding in a relationship. The question is: what motivates us as Christians – is it the need to perform well, or the desire for a relational dependence on God?

Paul, in Ephesians 2:8–9, shows us that we are made right with God by His grace, and we partake of that by faith, not performance. In Galatians, he further emphasises that just as we begin our relationship with God by grace through faith, we must continue as Christians on that basis (Galatians 3:3).

Anderson, Miller and Travis go on to give us a better definition of the Christian life, summed up as:

A personal, faith-relationship with God the Father through abiding in His Son, Jesus Christ, and walking in loving obedience to His Word through the person and power of the Holy Spirit.[2]

Being a Christian is about enjoying a relationship, it's not about keeping rules. If you never discover this, you will forever be locked into the repeated sequence of failure. Whilst boundaries, to a degree, may well be necessary to protect all of us from what is harmful, long-term, rules don't work. Rules may momentarily change our behaviour, but only deep relationship will change our hearts. Rules are about *doing*, relationship is about *being*. Essentially, it is the lack of *being* in all of us that causes us to gravitate towards the transitory pleasures of sin. Sadly, even some who recognise this try to remedy the problem by *doing* (or not *doing*), rather than *being*. Our rules and boundaries will never be enough. In fact, they make things worse. In Romans, Paul points out that God's Law, whilst perfect in itself, only served to aggravate the sin nature in him (Romans 7:8–9). It would appear that this sinful part in us becomes more resentful under the domination of the will, and rebels against all restrictions. Regulation brings to life the monster within all of us.

The two 'I's' – the open secret of holiness

The two 'I's' through which we receive the open secret of holiness are *identity* and *intimacy*. These have only appeared to be a secret because, for years, we have buried them under such a load of religious debris. Certainly, God is not guilty of having concealed these open secrets; on the contrary, He went to the greatest of lengths – giving His Son to die – in order that we should know them.

Identity is essentially knowing who we really are in Christ, as children of our Father.[3] Intimacy is the practical experience of closeness to God because of the relationship we now enjoy with Him. These two open secrets address the core reason people get stuck in sin – they have no sense of being. They don't know who they truly are and, therefore, they have no confidence to pursue a meaningful and satisfying relationship with God as their Father. Where there is no sense of being within, there will be no sense of worth. That lack of a sense of worth can be further compounded by our incessant failure to keep the rules (whatever those are for us).

It is our internal vacuity that makes sin so much more attractive to us. Sin either dulls the pain of the emptiness within us, or it gives a momentary 'feel-good factor', which provides a 'fix' for the vacuum of meaning inside. Unfortunately, as with any 'fix', the comedown leaves us feeling worse. 'Fixes' aren't the answer. The classic model of the addiction cycle illustrates this well. Usually pain seeks out pleasure, as I mentioned earlier. A person turns to a habit to deaden hurt. They get momentary relief through their vice, but then, when the buzz subsides, they are left with the original pain and an additional load of guilt and shame for having indulged in the illicit activity. What do they do now? The easiest and most accessible thing to do is to jump back into the cycle and indulge the 'quick fix' again. The only thing that will completely and permanently break this cycle is healing for the original wound. The pain that seeks the pleasure needs to be cured. Yes, confession and repentance are essential, but they may not be enough on their own if a gaping wound lies under the surface of the sinful habit.

A comprehensive gospel

The gospel of Jesus Christ is genuinely wholistic (in the literal sense of the word, not the New Age sense). The sacrifice of Jesus at the cross meets all our deepest needs. In other words, God is not only interested in some ethereal part of us (our spirit) that will live on forever in eternity, rather He is interested in the whole human being that He created – spirit, soul and body. In Christ, He has provided redemption for the entire person. Often evangelical Christians are guilty of restricting a great deal of the benefits of their salvation to the future age when, in fact, so much more than they ever imagined is available now!

God's intent in sending Jesus as our Saviour is declared in 1 Thessalonians 5:23–24. Eugene Peterson's *The Message* articulates it well:

May God himself, the God who makes everything holy and whole, make you holy and whole, put you together – spirit, soul, and body – and keep you fit for the coming of our Master, Jesus Christ. The One who called you is completely dependable. If he said it, he'll do it!

Many Christians have pursued a *holiness*, but without success because there is no *wholeness* in their lives. Then there are others who covet the 'quick fix' of *wholeness* and healing, but they are not prepared to answer the disciple's call to *holiness*. I'm afraid you cannot have one without the other. You cannot be *holy* without being *whole* and you cannot be *whole* without being *holy*. Are you ready for both? Do you desire both? This was always God's plan for us:

Long before he laid down earth's foundations, he had us in mind, had settled on us as the focus of his love, to be made whole and holy by his love. Long, long ago he decided to adopt us into his family through Jesus Christ. (What pleasure he took in planning this!) He wanted us to enter into the celebration of his lavish gift-giving by the hand of his beloved Son.

Ephesians 1:3–6 (The Message)

Sins must be confessed and repented of, but wounds cannot be repented of – they must be healed. Even where there is demonic empowerment involved in our sinful behaviours, deliverance is not enough if there are also hurts that need to be healed. The greatest healing begins with belonging: when we realise that God sent Jesus into the world to die in order to carry away our sin, so that we might come into God's family, be His sons and daughters, and call Him Father. Acceptance into God's family, knowing who we are in our new identity and abiding in that, will be the atmosphere where our healing and deliverance will be most effective. True holiness, as well as authentic wholeness, is found in relationship with Father.

On one occasion a pilot heard a gnawing noise in the fuselage of his plane during flight. He turned around and saw a rat chewing at some electric wires. The pilot knew the rodent was not made to withstand high altitudes, so he soared high in the sky, as high as he could go. After being up at that altitude for a number of minutes, he began his descent and landed the plane. When he searched the plane, he found the dead rat. In like manner, the only way to address persistent sin in your life is not to wrestle with it, or devise ingenious restraints for it – rather, the answer is to go higher into the heavenly atmosphere of relationship with your Father through Jesus. You must not be in denial or excuse your sin, we must all become present to the reality and extent of our sinful problems. However, having become present to our sin, we must not stay there. Some of us wallow morbidly in practising the presence of our sin. We must get sin, as it were, up and out of us through confession. Bring it up and out of us and, by faith, see it put upon Jesus who carried it away on the cross. When we do this by faith, and continue to do it, that great exchange can take place, as the divine sense of being comes down from Christ to us, filling our emptiness.

Let us be done once and for all with legalistic versions of Christianity – they don't work. Only 'the law of the Spirit of life in Christ Jesus' will deliver us 'from the law of sin and death' (Romans 8:2). The 'life of the Spirit' is God's own life filling our emptiness with His very Being; this is how true being and satisfying worth will come to our desolate hearts.

A Prayer

Lord Jesus, thank You that You came into the world to reveal the Father's love and plan for my life. You have shown me that it is God's will that I become holy and whole through relationship with You.

I confess all my sins and repent of them. I give them up to You, for You have taken them already upon the cross. I repent of all legalistic attempts to gain holiness apart from You, and I thank You that Your death on the cross and resurrection life is all I need to be holy.

I ask You to shine Your light on my unhealed parts that need Your wholeness. Fill my emptiness that so often seeks the 'quick fix' of sin. By Your Holy Spirit, reveal the Father's acceptance of me, and His unconditional love. Please lead me into a truly deep and meaningful relationship with Father, Son and Holy Spirit. Amen.[4]

———•———

1. Neil T. Anderson, Rich Miller, Paul Travis, *Breaking the Bondage of Legalism* (Eugene, OR: Harvest House Publishers, 2003).

2. Ibid.

3. As a resource to help in renewing the mind to your true identity in Christ, I would highly recommend Neil T. Anderson's devotional, *Living Free in Christ* (Oxford: Monarch Publications, 1993). Also, *Freedom in Christ* ministry's bookmark summary of *Who I Am in Christ*, which is available at www.freedominchrist.com (accessed 13.7.17).

4. Quite an extensive Lordship Prayer is available in the Appendix.

WOUNDS

He heals the brokenhearted
And binds up their wounds.
Psalm 147:3

CHAPTER FIVE
BROKEN HUMANITY

———◦———

We have established that sins must be repented of, wounds must be healed and demons must be expelled. The correct remedy must fit the particular problem. Misdiagnosis will likely result in mistreatment. This is the reason why the correct identification of our issues is vital: to ensure that we apply the right solution. Initially, I know it may appear an oversimplification to carve up our problems into these three areas. I don't want to give the impression that these categories are in isolation from one another; on the contrary, there is a great deal of overlap between them, as we shall see. Indeed, in most of our lives, there has been somewhat of a mixture of all three of these fields. However, for the purposes of clarity, these three distinctions are helpful in eradicating misunderstanding in relation to exactly where our real problems lie. For example, so many people have been trying to unsuccessfully repent for a sin without realising that the sin has actually been a coping mechanism for some underlying pain. Of course, as we have demonstrated, repentance is non-negotiable – it needs to happen for the freedom to come – but without healing for the underlying hurts, the chances of complete moral victory are very slim indeed.

The original wound

When Adam and Eve disobeyed God in Eden, their act of sin brought brokenness in its wake. Disorder entered the world as a whole, but it also seeped into the human soul. It is obvious how humankind's relationship with God was attacked by Satan's temptation and Adam's subsequent fall. Satan caused Adam and Eve to question the goodness of God and the trustworthiness of His Word. As a result of their disobedience, their special relationship with the Almighty received a devastating blow. Also, we observe that Adam and Eve's relationship with each other suffered a rift due to the way they started to blame each other for their own individual failures. However, what many readers of Genesis never consider is the personal brokenness that entered each person's relationship with themselves. A kind of fragmentation or dislocation took place within them.

Spirit, soul and body[1]

When God breathed into Adam and he came to life, it appears that God's breath imparted 'spirit' to Adam, which made him not only a creature formed from the earth's soil, but a being made in the image of God – a spiritual entity. At that moment, eternity was placed in the hearts of all humanity. This spirit would be the touchpoint between God and each human being, almost like a 'spiritual receiver' through which communication with God would be possible. It was to be through the spirit that God would influence the individual. If the spirit is the more 'God-conscious' part of the human, the soul appears to be the part which is more 'self-conscious'. Some have understood the soul to be comprised of the elements of the mind, the emotions and the will. Certainly, it is through our thoughts, feelings and actions that we express ourselves. Obviously, the body is the 'world-conscious' part of us that directly engages with our physical environment.

It appears that God's plan was to influence us in our spirits by His Spirit and then, through the thoughts, feelings and actions of our souls, prompt the body to behave in a way that glorified Him and accomplished His purposes. Of course, this plan was scuppered when men and women listened to the voice of the enemy and disobeyed God's perfect will for them. One of the consequences of this was that the spirit of each human being died. This does not mean that at that precise moment Adam dropped dead in Eden. Whilst the physical ageing process that advances death had begun, Adam was very much alive. Please note that death in the Bible does not mean 'to cease to exist', rather its fullest meaning is 'separation'. Adam's spirit remained intact when he sinned in the garden, the damage incurred was that his spirit came to be separated from God – the divine relationship was severed. The fact that all people still retain a spirit is an explanation for the spirituality we see all around the world, whether it be the various expressions of religious belief, or the occult and worship of Satan himself. There is a sense in which even the *complete unbeliever in anything* still has the propensity to worship themselves or the material objects they amass to make their lives feel worthwhile – these forms of idolatry also engage the spirit.

When the human spirit was divided from God, divine agency upon humanity was disrupted. Heaven's influence over humankind was obstructed. Consequently, the soul, which should have been shaped by God's Spirit affecting our spirit, became self-centred. The focal point of the mind, heart and volition became the self rather than God. As far as the body was concerned, instead of executing the will of God, it became sensual in obeying base appetites and the passions of the fallen self.

So, to summarise: the life in our spirit, where our true God-given identity is, is meant to be expressed through the thoughts, feelings and will of the soul, which in turn is carried out by the body. This explains why our thoughts, feelings and behaviours exhibit problems – something deeper is damaged. Being cut off from God means we have the ultimate identity crisis. When we live for ourselves rather than the creative purpose of living for God's glory, it is inevitable that we will eventually hit some kind of impasse.

Is it well with your soul?

Is your thought life troubling you? Are you exhibiting emotional distress? Are there behavioural patterns that are getting out of your control? All these are indicative of the fact that something buried deep within you is broken.

It is not only the soul that displays the giveaway signs of our spiritual brokenness, but also the body. Our deep heart wounds can physically manifest in the body.[2] It is a well-established fact that stress contributes to physical sickness. Medical professionals agree that mental and emotional problems are often at the root of illness – and, of course, we would factor in spiritual causes also. The minimum estimate is that 50 per cent of illness is psychosomatic,[3] and you will hear figures as high as 75 per cent quoted.[4]

The soul and body will reveal the spirit's condition. This may be indirectly hinted at in Hebrews 4:12–13:

For the word of God is living and active. Sharper than any double-edged sword, it penetrates even to dividing soul and spirit, joints and marrow; it judges the thoughts and attitudes of the heart. Nothing in all creation is hidden from God's sight. Everything is uncovered and laid bare before the eyes of him to whom we must give account.

(NIV 1984)

God's Word searches us completely, scanning us in order that the Great Physician should diagnose our condition. God is able to distinguish sins of the flesh from wounds of the heart. With surgical precision, the divine scalpel of God's Spirit is able to pinpoint exactly where our problems lie. We need to know what sins need to be repented of and what the wounds are that need healing. This discernment is vital. You may remember falling off your bicycle as a child and grazing your knee. Having run home to your mother for comfort, more than likely she took some antiseptic and cleansed your knee (making the pain momentarily worse) – why? – because dirt often gets into wounds and causes infection. Likewise, our brokenness can be a breeding ground for sinful behaviours in which the enemy can get a demonic foothold. Submitting to the Spirit of God through the Word of God will allow God to separate these in order to treat us.

Notice something further in Hebrews 4:12. There appears to be a linguistic parallel being made between 'soul' with 'joints', and 'spirit' with 'marrow'. The 'soul', like the 'joints', expresses life; but the 'spirit', like the 'marrow', is the *source* of life. If the spirit is damaged it will affect the whole person.

Using a similar analogy, Proverbs 17:22 states:

A merry heart does good, like medicine,
But a broken spirit dries the bones.

It appears that it is the spirit that sustains a person (or, for that matter, doesn't sustain them), rather than the soul. Again, Proverbs 18:14 reiterates that if our inner part is injured, the whole person will be struggling:

The spirit of a man will sustain him in sickness,
But who can bear a broken spirit?

Christ, the Healer

The good news of Jesus Christ is that on the cross He not only bore our sins, but He also bore our brokenness and our sorrows. Isaiah 53:5 proclaims:

But he was pierced for our transgressions,
he was crushed for our iniquities;
the punishment that brought us peace was upon him,
and by his wounds we are healed.

(NIV 1984)

The wounds that Jesus our Saviour bore on the cross have the power to heal our wounds and human brokenness.

Throughout His brief ministry on earth, our Lord constantly displayed His great compassion for those who found themselves crushed by shame and vicissitudes. He gave the immortal invitation to every overburdened soul:

Come to Me, all you who labor and are heavy laden, and I will give you rest. Take My yoke upon you and learn from

Me, for I am gentle and lowly in heart, and you will find rest
for your souls. For My yoke is easy and My burden is light.

Matthew 11:28–30

Healing our wounds was the declared prophetic mission
statement of the Messiah recorded in Isaiah 61:1–3:

The Spirit of the Lord God is upon Me,
Because the LORD has anointed Me
To preach good tidings to the poor;
He has sent Me to heal the brokenhearted,
To proclaim liberty to the captives,
And the opening of the prison to those who are bound;
To proclaim the acceptable year of the LORD,
And the day of vengeance of our God;
To comfort all who mourn,
To console those who mourn in Zion,
To give them beauty for ashes,
The oil of joy for mourning,
The garment of praise for the spirit of heaviness;
That they may be called trees of righteousness,
The planting of the LORD, that He may be glorified.

It is impossible for any of us to pass through this life without
incurring wounds. We all have them, the question is: what do
we do with them? Do we deny they exist? Do we ignore them
and hope they will disappear, only to find them raising their
grotesque head later in life? Do we try to stupefy them with some
thrill or addiction? Or do we bring them to the only One who
can truly help us in our human brokenness – Jesus Christ, the
Saviour of the human race?

A Prayer

Father, I acknowledge that when You created humankind, You created us in Your image. Having made us, You declared that we were 'very good'.[5] However, it was our disobedience that marred Your creation.

Likewise, it has been my sin and the sins of others against me that have brought brokenness to my spirit, soul and body. I thank You that because You love me, You sent Your Son Jesus into this world to be my Saviour, and when He died on the cross He bore all my pain and suffering. I believe and declare that His wounds are sufficient to heal my wounds.

I ask You, Father, to gently lead me on the path of revelation and disclose to me those parts of me that are broken and bruised and in need of Your healing touch. Father, I choose to trust You to apply Your healing to my wounds in the power of the Holy Spirit. Amen.

---

1. Some understand the make-up of a human being to be spirit, soul and body, but others understand us only to be made of an immaterial part: soul/spirit, and a material part: the body. There is no doubt that there is some overlap in Scripture between the terms 'soul' and 'spirit' but many believe, myself included, that there are grounds to understand certain distinctions between the spirit and the soul.

2. No one should misconstrue that I am saying that all illness is spiritual, it is clearly not; however, some is.

3. Psychosomatic does not mean that an illness is imaginary and all in your mind; rather, it refers to actual physical symptoms that have either mental or emotional origins.

4. These figures are quoted in Neil and Joanne Anderson, *Overcoming Depression* (Ventura, CA: Regal, 2004).

5. Genesis 1:31.

CHAPTER SIX
HAPPILY EVER AFTER?

———•———

Playing 'Happy Families' is a thing of fairy tales for many. In these next few chapters, we will be exploring the question of how and where we can become wounded. The general answer to this question is: we can be wounded from *anywhere* by *anyone*! That covers a lot of potential sources of injury. Narrowing it down a little, probably the most common channel of wounding is via our families and our friends. Previously, we observed that not only was humanity's relationship with God broken through the fall into sin, but also affected was their relationship with each other. A great deal of our brokenness comes to us as a result of our relationships. Both the highest and the lowest points in life tend to revolve around relationships; the best of times and the worst of times. The reward of relationship is love, but often the price is pain. Relationship is the place where we risk rejection.

From conception

Some might think it fanciful nonsense to suggest that a person can be wounded from the very moment of their conception; but why could this not be the case? If, indeed, life starts at conception by receiving within us a God-breathed spirit (the place where our identity lies), and if that spirit is like a receiver that picks up all sorts of signals, is it completely inconceivable that the child in the womb could be influenced by the behaviours of their parents, or the conditions of their environment?

In Luke 1:41–44, we read that when the pregnant virgin Mary visited her pregnant older cousin Elizabeth, the unborn John the Baptist leapt for joy in Elizabeth's womb – presumably because he was in the presence of his Lord, Jesus, in Mary's womb. Of course, John's brain was not fully formed, nor his emotions matured, so where then did John detect the presence of Jesus? Surely, it must have been in that part of him designed to respond to God – his spirit.

Scientific medical research has now well established that the child in the womb responds better in its development whenever there is affirmation and positive interaction with its environment. Pregnant mothers are encouraged to play music to, read stories to, and positively affirm the unborn child. It is believed that from this, the child will derive more of a sense of security and well-being. Surely it figures then that the reverse will be true: where the baby in the womb has a hostile and toxic surrounding, it will be adversely affected. Children are often described as being like 'sponges' in the manner in which they soak up information all around them. The spirit is like a sponge soaking up both positive and negative communications.

Many wounded people have not appreciated the extent to which the circumstances of their conception or gestation in the womb have impacted them. For instance, some people who have experienced a sense of rejection for as long as they can remember may have been a child of an unwanted pregnancy. Derek Prince once discovered, when ministering to people in the USA, that commonly those in a certain age group seemed to have a sense of early rejection. When he traced it back, he discovered that many of these people had been born during the Great Depression (1929–30). He began to understand that at that time, parents with many mouths to feed could hardly bear the thought of one more, so this inner attitude of rejection wounded the unborn child.[1]

Imagine the potential damage to a child if the circumstances of their conception were rape, or some other abusive or controlling relationship. Consider the harm incurred if a child was born after surviving a failed abortion attempt. Even situations that appear less serious than these can still have devastating effects. For example, a mother who is particularly ill or anxious during pregnancy may unintentionally convey a sense of insecurity to the child. It is then possible that fear may become a dominating influence in the child's life. Or, if either parent during pregnancy constantly expresses their preference for a boy or a girl and is then disappointed with the gender of the child when it is born, what do you think such disappointment might do to the child's identity or sense of acceptance?

Parents

Our parents are the two people who make the biggest impact on our formation as persons (whether or not they have both been around). A child often discovers what kind of person they are and how to think and feel about themselves from their parents' reaction to them. A significant number of counsellors believe that the majority of a child's identity is formed particularly through the father-child relationship. It is also true that a person's concept of God will often be moulded by their relationship with their dad. Our parents are meant to be signposts that point to the ultimate parent: God the Father. When our parents do a bad job, particularly fathers, what do you think happens to our perception of God? You guessed it: it gets damaged.

As a concept, fatherhood and masculinity are not highly valued in our modern-day society. As a result, it is suffering both moral and spiritual meltdown. We are, if ever there was one, 'the fatherless generation'. Surely this is the major social crisis of the Western world. The nuclear family is seriously under threat. It has been recorded that Britain has the highest divorce rate in the European Union,[2] whilst in the USA divorce statistics are little different among Christians than among non-believers.[3]

The good news is that according to Malachi 4:6, God has promised in these end times that:

> ... he will turn the hearts of the fathers to the children,
> And the hearts of the children to their fathers,
> Lest I come and strike the earth with a curse.

It is the case that wherever a father's heart is turned towards anything other than his children, a curse can be released – not only on the family, but the land.

So, how has your relationship with your parents been? Did you have an absent or distant parent? Were they controlling or abusive? Did they reject you, or cause you fear? Did they require you to earn their favour? Did your parents know how to express love? Were they tactile and verbally affirming? Some parents put too much responsibility on their children. Perhaps your parents were broken themselves and looked to you to supply their emotional needs. Many children have never been taught true love and therefore don't know how to express it or receive it. Many people will testify, 'Of course, I know my mum and dad loved me, they just never told me.'

Perhaps, for you, it wasn't so much the case that your parents didn't know how to love you, but rather that they showed favouritism towards your sibling. A quick look at the book of Genesis will show the damage that sibling rivalry can do (i.e. Jacob's preference of Joseph). Derek Prince tells the story of a mother who had several daughters but favoured one. One day she heard a sound in another room. Thinking it was the daughter she loved most, she called out, 'Is that you, darling?' The discouraged voice of the other daughter replied, 'No, it's only me!'[4] How devastating it is when a parent overlooks one child in favour of another.

Please note, our objective here is not to pin the blame for all our dysfunctional issues on our parents. As we saw in the opening chapters of this book, we must take ownership of our own ungodly behaviours; blaming others is not an option. Also, we are instructed in the fifth commandment[5] to honour our fathers and mothers, and we must do this, even if the only thing we might be able to honour them for is giving us life. We must be open before God to the possibility that we have misread our parents' dealings with us and *we* have got it wrong. How much of our interpretation of past events is fact and how much is merely our impression? How much of our reaction to our parents' behaviour was tempered by our rebelliousness or other sinful influences that we were under at the time?

On the other hand, some Christians get scared that by admitting shortcomings in their parents they will be dishonouring them and transgressing the fifth commandment. This is not the case at all. There is nothing dishonourable in conceding the truth. None of us *are* perfect parents, and none of us have *had* perfect parents. The only perfect parent is God the Father. As long as we are being honest concerning what has taken place in our experience with our parents, we have no cause for concern. Providing we deal with the matter before God and a few confidants, with integrity and without judgement or slander towards our parents, we have nothing to worry about. In fact, it is imperative that we don't suppress such matters but bring them into the open before God for healing.

Friends and acquaintances

When we have close relationships with people, heart ties (or soul ties) can be established. It was always God's intention for this to be the case. A heart tie is a source of blessing when under godly order. This can be seen in God's design for the sacred union of marriage from Genesis 2:24:

Therefore a man shall leave his father and mother and be joined to his wife, and they shall become one flesh.

However, when there is not godly order in a relationship, the heart tie can become a negative source of influence that harms a person. Surely such associations were in Paul's mind when he wrote in 2 Corinthians 6:14–15:

Do not be unequally yoked together with unbelievers. For what fellowship has righteousness with lawlessness? And what communion has light with darkness? And what accord has Christ with Belial? Or what part has a believer with an unbeliever?

The farmers' yoke is a very graphic depiction of what a heart tie does. It joins us in soul to another in either a healthy or an unhealthy way.

A biblical example of a positive heart tie would be the friendship between David and Jonathan. First Samuel 18:1 says:

> ... the soul of Jonathan was knit to the soul of David, and Jonathan loved him as his own soul.

Another example, this time from the New Testament, is that of the close bond that believers are to have in the fellowship of the Church body. Paul exhorts in Colossians 2:1–2:

> For I want you to know what a great conflict I have for you and those in Laodicea, and for as many as have not seen my face in the flesh, that their hearts may be encouraged, being knit together in love ...

Christian fellowship is a spiritual union of hearts knit together through the love of God.

Alternatively, a negative example of a heart tie would be the relationship of the father, Jacob, with his son, Benjamin. There appears to have been an unhealthy co-dependency to the point of being a threat to Jacob's life. When Joseph requested that Benjamin remain in Egypt with him, Judah makes this plea recorded in Genesis 44:22, 30–31:

> The lad cannot leave his father, for if he should leave his father, his father would die ... Now therefore when I come to your servant my father, and the lad is not with us, since his life is bound up in the lad's life, it will happen, when

he sees that the lad is not with us, that he will die. So your servants will bring down the gray hair of your servant our father with sorrow to the grave.

What a telling expression, that Jacob's life was unhealthily 'bound up' or 'wrapped up' in the life of his favourite son, Benjamin.

Of course, one of the strongest spiritual ties for people appears to be the sexual union (indeed, any sexual activity). This is a God-ordained, positive experience of bonding in marriage. However, when sexual activity takes place outside the boundary of God's order (marriage) such ties become destructive. No doubt this is part of what Paul had in mind when he warned in 1 Corinthians 6:15–18:

Do you not know that your bodies are members of Christ? Shall I then take the members of Christ and make them the members of a harlot? Certainly not! Or do you not know that he who is joined to a harlot is one body with her? For 'the two,' He says, 'shall become one flesh.' But he who is joined to the Lord is one spirit with Him. Flee sexual immorality. Every sin that a man does is outside the body, but he who commits sexual immorality sins against his own body.

In the light of these verses, no one could conclude that there is such a thing as 'casual sex'. All sexual activity outside the safe bounds of a loving and selfless marriage is dangerous. Even when sexual relations are not at all abusive but completely consensual, the enemy knows how to tie us in relational knots. The actual relationship may have ended years previously, and perhaps we have moved into a subsequent relationship, yet we may still remain tied in some way to the previous person through the historic sexual contact.

It is amazing how, without realising it, even our popular love songs can betray this truth. Aretha Franklin sang the song, 'Piece of My Heart' and in later years Paul Young sang, 'Every Time You Go Away', both songs reflecting the idea of broken pieces of the heart being left with lovers. It is very possible that presently you are experiencing brokenness because of a past relationship.

Other unhealthy relationships can bring about a soul tie: abuse, bullying, destructive friendships, passive aggression, idolatry, secret societies, forbidden activity with the occult or New Age practitioners, controlling religious/church leaders, and even false prophecy or false pronouncements. All of these are relationships where there is the potential for the forming of a damaging spiritual tie.

Who would ever have thought that our interactions with other human beings could have such a deep spiritual impact on us? If we are to know healing for all our wounds, we must be real about the practical implications of past and present relationships. Only then can there be the needed honesty for the Lord to meet us at the point of truth with His marvellous grace.

A Prayer

Abba Father, thank You that You are the One True Father, after whom every family in heaven and earth has been named.

I ask You to reveal to me all earthly relationships, past or present, that have harmed me. Please give me the grace to forgive those who have hurt me.

Also, Father, I ask You to please break any ungodly ties there may be with anyone I have been wrongly joined to (*be specific and name these people if you can*).

Please heal me now of all damage from every unhealthy relationship. Thank You, Father. Amen.

————•————

1. Derek Prince, *God's Remedy for Rejection* (New Kensington, PA: Whitaker House, 1993).

2. Daily Mail Online, 12 June 2017.

3. Jack Frost, *Experiencing Father's Embrace* (Shippensburg, PA: Destiny Image Publishers, 2002).

4. Derek Prince, *God's Remedy for Rejection.*

5. Exodus 20:12.

CHAPTER SEVEN
THE TIME TRAP

We have been exploring the various ways we can receive wounds which hinder us in moving on to freedom in Christ. Another very common and debilitating barrier to blessing is the experience of being caught in some historical event. Through an accident or some other traumatic incident, a person can get – as it were – 'stuck' in the pain and, no matter what they attempt to do, they seem unable to move on from it.

Tied up in the past

In his Gospel, Luke the doctor records for us the healing of a woman in the synagogue who had a spirit of infirmity. She was in the synagogue on the Sabbath worshipping, and Jesus Himself refers to her as:

> ... a daughter of Abraham, whom Satan has bound – think of it – for eighteen years ...

This language would appear to indicate that this lady was a woman of faith, a believer, and yet she was afflicted by some bondage from Satan; specifically, a spirit of infirmity, causing her to be physically bent over for eighteen years. It is interesting how detailed Luke is in recording that this woman became afflicted eighteen years previously. It appears that something happened to this woman eighteen years before that 'bound' her with a spirit of infirmity that now required both healing and deliverance.[1] This predicament would account for the choice of language Jesus used when healing the woman. Luke 13:12 records:

> He called her to Him and said to her, 'Woman, you are loosed from your infirmity.' And He laid His hands on her, and immediately she was made straight, and glorified God.

Jesus' use of the term 'loosed' as well as 'bound' (verse 16) would infer that she had been tied up in bondage by the enemy eighteen years before and that her sickness was the fruit of this. Remember, Jesus was not simply healing this woman of a sickness. He did do that, of course, but this woman could only be healed after being delivered of a spirit of sickness. Luke clearly recounts that Jesus 'loosed' her and then laid hands on her for healing.

The illustration Jesus then uses to answer the ruler of the synagogue's objection to Him healing on the Sabbath further confirms this impression. In Luke 13:15–16 Jesus says:

> Hypocrite! Does not each one of you on the Sabbath loose his ox or donkey from the stall, and lead it away to water it? So ought not this woman, being a daughter of Abraham, whom Satan has bound – think of it – for eighteen years, be loosed from this bond on the Sabbath?

The imagery of loosing an animal from a tie is unmistakeably alluding to the loosing of this woman from demonic bondage.

So to summarise, here is a lady who, eighteen years before (through circumstances unknown to us), received a spirit of infirmity, bringing her into spiritual bondage that manifested in sickness. In order for this woman to be healed, Jesus looses her (or unties her) from the past spiritual anchorage, delivering her of the demon and healing her of the sickness.

So, it is possible to get entangled by our personal histories. We can become attached to people, places or events that moor us to a distant shore, preventing us moving on.

Caught in time

Dr D. Martyn Lloyd-Jones, who ministered for many years at Westminster Chapel in London, recounts the story of being in his native Wales preaching in the early 1930s when, after an afternoon service, two ministers came and asked him for a favour.[2] They told him of the tragic case of the local schoolmaster, a very fine man, whom they said was one of the best church workers in the district but who was now in a very sad condition. He had given up all his church work and managed only to attend his work at school. Dr Lloyd-Jones asked what exactly was wrong with him. They replied that he had some depressive condition and complained of headaches and pains in his stomach. The ministers asked if Dr Lloyd-Jones, who previously had been a physician, would be kind enough to meet with him. He agreed and, after tea, the man arrived. The moment Dr Lloyd-Jones saw him, he said: 'You look depressed... Now tell me, what's the trouble?'

'Well,' he said, 'I get these headaches, I'm never free from them. I wake up with one in the morning, and I can't sleep too well either.' He added that he also suffered from gastric pains and various other complaints.

Dr Lloyd-Jones asked him, 'Tell me, how long have you been like this?'

'Oh,' he said, 'it's been going on for years. As a matter of fact, it's been going on since 1915.'

'I'm interested to hear this,' said Dr Lloyd-Jones. 'How did it begin?'

He said, 'Well, when the war broke out in 1914, I volunteered very early on and went into the navy. Eventually I transferred to a submarine, which was sent to the Mediterranean. Now, the part of the navy I belonged to was involved in the Gallipoli Campaign. I was there in this submarine in the Mediterranean during that campaign. One afternoon we were engaged in action. We were submerged in the sea, and we were all engaged in our duties when suddenly there was a most terrible thud and our submarine shook. We'd been hit by a mine, and down we sank to the bottom of the Mediterranean. You know, since then I've never been the same man.'

'Well,' said Dr Lloyd-Jones, 'please tell me the rest of your story.'

'But,' said the schoolmaster, 'there's really nothing more to say. I'm just telling you that's how I've been ever since that happened to me in the Mediterranean.'

'But, my dear friend,' said Dr Lloyd-Jones, 'I really would be interested to know the remainder of the story.'

'But I've told you the whole story!'

This went on for some considerable time. Dr Lloyd-Jones asked again, 'Now I really would like to know the whole story. Start at the beginning again.'

The schoolmaster recounted the story several times about how he was posted to a submarine that went to the Mediterranean, and everything was all right until the afternoon they were engaged in the action, the sudden thud and the shaking. 'Down we went to the bottom of the Mediterranean. And I have been like this ever since.'

After many times reciting his account, the schoolmaster insisted, 'There's nothing more to be said.'

Dr Lloyd-Jones then asked the schoolmaster this incisive question: 'Are you still at the bottom of the Mediterranean?' Dr Lloyd-Jones explains that, physically, the man was not at the bottom of the Mediterranean, yet mentally he was. In his mind, he had remained at the bottom of the Mediterranean ever since.

Dr Lloyd-Jones continued to explain to the schoolmaster, 'That's your whole trouble. All your troubles are due to the fact that, in your own mind, you are still at the bottom of the Mediterranean. Why didn't you tell me that somehow or another you came up to the surface, that someone on another ship saw you, got hold of you and got you on board his ship, that you were treated there and eventually brought back to England and put into a hospital? ... You stopped at the bottom of the Mediterranean.'

This man was loosed from the Mediterranean through Dr Lloyd-Jones' intervention and was completely restored. He resumed his duties in the church and within a year he had applied for ordination in the Anglican Church in Wales.

The power of past trauma cannot be underestimated. Post-Traumatic Stress Disorder (PTSD) is a case in point. Soldiers return from the battlefield and perhaps, over time, bodily injuries may mend – yet their minds, hearts and spirits can remain deeply fractured.

All of us have the potential of being fastened to our traumatic memories and held back from enjoying the fullness of our destiny in Christ.

Miss Havisham from Charles Dickens' novel *Great Expectations* epitomises someone caught in time. She was the daughter of a very wealthy man and, on the morning of her wedding day at 8:40am, she received a letter relaying the message that her husband-to-be was not coming. Dickens depicts Miss Havisham as stopping all clocks in the house at the precise time the letter arrived. She spends the rest of her life in her bridal gown, which eventually turns yellow with age. She only wears one shoe, since she had not put the other one on at the time of the catastrophe. Even as an elderly woman, she remained crippled by the burden of this devastating calamity.

Are you in a time trap, caught in some traumatic event, unable to move on? It is possible to not even realise this is the case. When circumstances appear to get better, difficult people move out of our lives, and broken bodies heal, we can assume that the trouble is past. Time may have passed, but we may not have moved on from the effects of our experiences.

When I teach on this issue of trauma I often show a slide of a stick man with bandages on his eye and his leg. On a couple of occasions that simple picture has brought a kind of revelation to some people that there has been an accident, an illness or a serious surgical procedure that they have recovered from in a physical sense but not mentally, emotionally and spiritually.

The healing of memories

Jesus Christ is given the title 'the Alpha and Omega, the Beginning and the End' in Revelation 1:8. Daniel describes God as 'the Ancient of Days' (Daniel 7:9). Jesus our Saviour, as the Eternal Son of God, is not bound to the confines of time. This is incredible news for anyone trapped in traumatic memories. It means that Jesus can, as it were, come with us into the past and release us from those harmful memories. He can loose us from the destructive ties of the past.

It should be noted that God doesn't change our past. Created order is such that this is not possible. However, what God can do is redeem the past by healing our memories. Perhaps you have been driving yourself mad trying, with futility, to forget those painful memories. Or it may be that you are tormented by flashbacks or nightmares you have found impossible to eradicate. It is possible that you need these memories healed.

We will be addressing the important subject of forgiveness later in this book, but sometimes some people find it almost impossible to forgive others who have harmed them, because the memories are not healed. They do want to forgive, but their unhealed traumatic memories associated with an offender prevent them from doing so.

If you need your memories healed, it is vital that you are not in denial about them, or seeking to bury them – that won't work. What actually needs to happen is that you become present to the memory or memories in God's presence. I mean that in the safe and secure place of God's love and protection, you allow the difficult memory to surface and then ask the Lord Jesus – who is not bound by time – to take your hand and go with you to that difficult place, breaking the power of the memory. Please note, I am not suggesting that you drag up old memories that are not troubling you significantly, nor am I encouraging you to entirely relive an atrocity in your mind in a way that would result in your retraumatisation. Rather, become present to the part of the memory that is bearable enough – for instance, just after the traumatic event. Ask Jesus to come with you to that place. Then, in your mind's eye, still present in the memory, watch for Jesus; watch what He will do or what He might say. This can be very powerful for many, as Jesus appears or speaks in such a way that breaks the power of the memory. This intervention of Jesus then becomes the conclusion of the memory. Whenever the memory surfaces again, this will be remembered as the ending of the memory and its point of closure. This may not happen for everyone, particularly if the imaginative faculties have shut down,[3] but more often than not this simple exercise brings an amazing break with the past. Some of the most beautiful healings I have ever witnessed have been when Jesus Himself tenderly interacts with a traumatised soul and looses them from the poisonous power of a tormenting memory.

A Prayer

Lord Jesus, Lord of all time, Alpha and Omega, search my past and disclose to me any way in which I am bound to people, places, organisations or events associated with accidents or traumas. Please loose me from anything of this nature that binds me.

I ask You to heal me of the mental, emotional, physical and spiritual wounds derived from these traumas. I bring to You any harmful memories which still haunt me today. As I become present to them, I ask You to take my hand, go with me to that place and release me from the power of this memory. I now wait, I look and listen for what You will do or say.

Thank You, Lord Jesus, that on the cross You endured all my suffering so that I could receive Your healing. Amen.

—————•————

1. It is instructive to note how, at times in the Gospels, the term 'healing' is used to refer to deliverances from demonic spirits. Deliverance was part of the healing ministry of Jesus.

2. This story is paraphrased from the original sermon recording of Dr Martyn Lloyd-Jones, www.mljtrust.org/sermons/a-picture-of-the-church/ (accessed 10.8.17).

3. Whilst this is something that can be tried on your own, in many cases it would be better to be assisted by someone experienced in prayer ministry.

CHAPTER EIGHT
THE SELF-DESTRUCT BUTTON

———٠———

We have considered several external contributing factors to personal wounding, but now we must focus our attention on a major internal factor: the tendency to turn against ourselves and press the self-destruct button.

The root of rejection

All of us have experienced rejection of one kind or another, whether it is failing an exam, not gaining a university place, not making the school team, or being dumped by a boyfriend or girlfriend. In this book, we have already reflected upon how human relationships open up great potential for hurt and pain. In particular, the scars of rejection run deep for many of us. Perhaps you have sensed rejection from your parents? Others have received rejection because of a marriage break-up – and, if that break-up was due to unfaithfulness, there can also be the sense of betrayal, further compounding that rejection. Some people regularly face rejection in the form of racial or religious prejudice, whilst others experience it in the school, college, or workplace as bullying and intimidation. Rejection is an inevitable part of life which can take many different forms. How are you experiencing it? If you have ever desired to belong and fit in, but you have always felt unaccepted or unwanted, then you have experienced rejection. Rejection can seriously damage your health. Some people have never faced their rejection – perhaps it's so deep that they don't even know it's there – but, in all likelihood it's affecting them in some way every day of their lives.

Rejection is one of the most common roots of many personal problems. Derek Prince described how, when he first began ministering to people with addictions, he quickly discovered that rejection was at the root of their problems. He said:

I discovered that addictions ... are merely twigs sprouting from a bigger branch. Normally the branch that supports them is some form of frustration. The practical solution, therefore, is to deal with the branch. When the branch of frustration is cut off, dealing with the twigs of addiction is relatively easy.

As I continued to wrestle with people's personal problems, I gradually worked my way down to the trunk of the tree until I came to the part of the tree that lies below the surface – that is, the roots. It is here that God seeks to work in our lives.

From where is the tree cut down? From the roots. When I got down below the surface, I made a discovery that surprised me at first. One of the most common roots of all personal problems is rejection.[1]

The pain of rejection is the origin of so many of our problems, not least our inability to properly connect with God. Rejection is one of the greatest hindrances to us experiencing God's love in all its fullness.

Self-rejection

Two common fruits that rejection produces are fear of rejection and self-rejection. Self-rejection usually comes from reasoning that if others don't value us, then why should we have any regard for ourselves? This results in a crippling low self-esteem. Self-loathing, manifesting in various forms of self-harm, is very common today right across our society; the ultimate demonstration of self-rejection being suicide.

You may never have contemplated suicide or self-harm, but self-rejection may be exhibited in your life through self-talk. Self-talk is what you say in your own head about yourself. Take a moment to examine the kinds of things you say to yourself about yourself. What kind of language do you use? Are your words constructive, or destructive? Do your pronouncements agree more with God's view of your existence, or the enemy's? Do you ever use words towards yourself such as 'ugly', 'useless', 'failure', 'stupid', or 'not good enough'?

When we come into agreement with the enemy's view of us, we co-operate with his agenda for our personal destruction. Satan is described as being our 'accuser' (Revelation 12:10). I'm sure, at times, the devil could take a vacation – because, in our own heads, we carry on his work for him! I know that for many people, cruel words were first spoken over them by another person. However, over time, such impressions of themselves have become engrained in their own psyche and the echo of those damaging words has formed a repetitive self-commentary that has devastated their self-worth.

Identity crisis

Every human is created in the image of God and therefore possesses value.[2] The source of all identity crisis is the confusion caused by the lies that Satan tells us about God and ourselves. Adam and Eve were the first to be subjected to this deception from the serpent when he questioned God's destiny for humanity.[3] Satan is the original identity thief. He is always tempting us to seek knowledge and significance apart from God.[4] It is sin (our disobedience to God's will for our lives) and our alienation from God (who gave us our identity in the first place) that has caused our identity confusion. This confusion of identity has given rise to questions like: 'Who am I?', 'What am I worth?', and 'What is the point of my life?' Satan's objective is to distort and destroy the image of God in us.

Divine worth

Healing from rejection, and specifically self-rejection, begins when you realise you were created with worth in the divine image. Yes, sin has damaged that image, but through Jesus and His death and resurrection we can be redeemed and made new. God has created us with worth, and the good news is: He has never lost sight of who He created us to be.

There may be many things you don't like about yourself, but you need to hear God's commentary on how you were made. Psalm 139:13–18:

> For you created my inmost being;
> you knit me together in my mother's womb.
> I praise you because I am fearfully and wonderfully made;
> your works are wonderful,
> I know that full well.

My frame was not hidden from you
when I was made in the secret place,
when I was woven together in the depths of the earth.
Your eyes saw my unformed body;
all the days ordained for me were written in your book
before one of them came to be.
How precious to me are your thoughts, God!
How vast is the sum of them!
Were I to count them,
they would outnumber the grains of sand –
when I awake, I am still with you.

(NIV UK 2011)

You are not a mistake, whatever the circumstances of your conception were. You are not a misfit or a freak, whatever your struggles in life have been. When God created the world of nature He declared it 'good', but it wasn't until He made humankind in His image that He proclaimed that everything He had made was 'very good'.[5] The human being was the pinnacle of His creation. David the psalmist is declaring with divine self-worth: 'God made me well! He did a good job when He made me!' Can you say that? This is not pride if we are finding our worth in God and not ourselves alone.

One of our greatest problems is that we integrate our sinful traits or ungodly behaviours into our identity. We say, 'This is who I am', when really it is only what we do. Sinful patterns are often never broken because we have made them part of our identity. We need to reject this lie and see ourselves as God sees us, not only in creation but in our redemption – who Jesus has made us to be in Him. Most Christians continue to live out of a broken picture of how they see themselves, long after their identity has been changed in Christ.

Demolishing strongholds

The voice you listen to and submit to will be the force that moulds you. Many of us have been moulded by lies. These lies have become established as strongholds in our minds. These strongholds exhibit themselves in our belief systems about life in general and our own personal lives. What is the lie you have believed about yourself, about your circumstances, or even about God and His ways towards you? We need to identify these strongholds of lies and confront them with the truth of what God says about us in the power of the Spirit. Paul encourages us in 2 Corinthians 10:4–5:

> For the weapons of our warfare are not carnal but mighty in God for pulling down strongholds, casting down arguments and every high thing that exalts itself against the knowledge of God, bringing every thought into captivity to the obedience of Christ ...

We must replace the lies of the enemy with the truth and seek to constantly protect that truth in the future. This is not a one-off exercise, but the renewal of the mind must be the ongoing experience of the Christian. The battlefield where Satan wages his warfare is the battlefield of the mind. You must take the battle to him with the sword of the Spirit – the specific Word given to you from God to deliver you from the devil's attack.

Our new identity

The sure remedy for all problems of rejection and tendencies towards self-destruction is to stand firm in our reborn identity in Christ. The Bible says we are 'new creations' in Christ (see 2 Corinthians 5:17). God now sees us in Christ. Paul says in Colossians 3:1–3:

If then you were raised with Christ, seek those things which are above, where Christ is, sitting at the right hand of God. Set your mind on things above, not on things on the earth. For you died, and your life is hidden with Christ in God.

We need to adopt the heavenly perspective on our position, hidden in Jesus, who is hidden in God. Our reborn identity is: we are God's children and He is our Father, our sins are completely forgiven and we have been accepted by God and belong to Him. Ephesians 1:6 says:

He made us accepted in the Beloved.

In Christ, we are acceptable to God – so is it not time we accepted ourselves? I don't mean that we nonchalantly accept sinful behaviours in our lives, but rather we accept who Christ has made us to be. Incidentally, our true identity in Christ will be the first thing that will give us victory over our sins. Identity is the key. Neil Anderson highlighted this when he taught: what we do does not determine who we are, but who we are determines what we do.[6]

How you see yourself is crucial. If you simply see yourself as a helpless sinner, what else are you going to do only help yourself to sin? You'll sin by faith, as it were, because that is what you *believe* you are. However, if you believe you are who God says you are and that you have at your disposal what He says you have, when sinful temptation comes knocking at your door, you will remember your identity and reason: 'This is not who I am, so this is not what I do!'

So, how do you see yourself? In Judges 6:11–16, God saw Gideon as a mighty man of courage and called him such – much to Gideon's incredulity, because at that moment he was hiding in fear from the Midianite enemy. To me, Gideon didn't look brave at all; but I don't see as God sees. God doesn't just see the raw material before Him, but the potential of what He can make a man or woman become if they surrender to His love. Gideon *did* become a brave warrior of renown who did great exploits for the Lord.

On one occasion, the young Michelangelo was given some rather unsatisfactory raw material, a marble block which had lain neglected for twenty-five years in the courtyard of Florence Cathedral. Two artists had previously tried to make a sculpture from the marble to no avail. By now, the marble had been overexposed to the elements and was weather-beaten. It was reported that Michelangelo was not very happy with the material he had been given, but as it was too expensive to dispose of, he went to work. I have often heard it said that when Michelangelo looked at that ugly block of rough marble, he did not see mere misshapen and weathered stone but he saw the completed statue of David – the finished work.

If you could picture yourself as an unworked piece of marble – what do you see? Hopelessness, or eternal potential because of the Divine Sculptor?

Is it not time to stop co-operating with the devil's agenda of destruction on your life and co-operate with God's eternal purpose for your destiny?

God knew what he was doing from the very beginning. He decided from the outset to shape the lives of those who love him along the same lines as the life of his Son. The Son stands first in the line of humanity he restored. We see the original and intended shape of our lives there in him. After

God made that decision of what his children should be like, he followed it up by calling people by name. After he called them by name, he set them on a solid basis with himself. And then, after getting them established, he stayed with them to the end, gloriously completing what he had begun.

Romans 8:29–30 (The Message)

A Prayer

Father, I thank You that You created me with dignity and purpose. I acknowledge that I have been made in Your image with value and worth.

I confess that sin has marred Your image in me. Forgive the times when I have co-operated with Satan in destroying that image, whether through disobedience or listening to his lies. I renounce those lies now (*specify what the lies are if you can*) and I replace them with the truth (*replace the lie with the corresponding truth of what God says*).

Please heal me of all rejection. Help me to forgive those who have rejected me and forgive me for any self-rejection. Also, forgive me if my self-rejection has progressed to self-harm or even attempts to take my own life.

I choose to accept my true identity as You have made me (apart from my sin, of course) and my reborn identity in the Lord Jesus Christ. Please, Father, I ask You to renew my mind according to Your truth, so that I would view myself as You see me. Thank You that this is now possible because of Jesus living in me. Amen.

———•———

1. Derek Prince, *God's Remedy for Rejection.*

2. Genesis 1:26.

3. Genesis 3:1.

4. Genesis 3:4–5.

5. Genesis 1:31.

6. Neil T. Anderson, *Living Free in Christ* (Oxford: Monarch Publications, 1993).

CHAPTER NINE
THE GOD OF RESCUE

———·———

God wants to redeem what Satan has sought to destroy. God sent His Son, Jesus Christ into the world on a mission to 'heal the brokenhearted' (Isaiah 61:1). In His earthly ministry, Jesus invited burdened sinners to come to Him to find rest (Matthew 11:28–30). Matthew 12:20 declares that Jesus fulfilled the prophetic description of the Servant of the Lord from Isaiah 42:3:

A bruised reed He will not break,
And smoking flax He will not quench …

Imagine a bulrush, broken and hanging by a sinew, in the midst of other bulrushes standing tall and straight. If you are broken and just hanging by a thread, Jesus is not the kind of person who comes along and snaps you in half, but rather He comes to rescue and restore you. Imagine, after dinner, blowing out the flame of a table candle. The rising smoke betrays the presence of the last dying embers of the fire. When our life is almost burned to ashes and there are only smoking embers left, Jesus is not the kind of person to lick His thumb and forefinger and extinguish all that remains of heat and light. No, He wants to fan life to flame, and set a fire of *true* life in us that is all-consuming.

Many broken people turn to empty religion for an answer, only to find that it increases the burdens upon them. Don't make the mistake that many do of attempting to exchange the burden of their sin and hurt for the burden of crushing religious slavery. Man-made religion will only exacerbate your problems and give you more scars that need healing. Jesus actually called people away from futile legalism to abundant life:

> Are you tired? Worn out? Burned out on religion? Come to me. Get away with me and you'll recover your life. I'll show you how to take a real rest. Walk with me and work with me – watch how I do it. Learn the unforced rhythms of grace. I won't lay anything heavy or ill-fitting on you. Keep company with me and you'll learn to live freely and lightly.
> *Matthew 11:28–30 (The Message)*

God wants to set us free from all unnecessary burdens and heal us from every wound. As we saw previously, this was always God's intention. Paul said in 1 Thessalonians 5:23–24:

> May God himself, the God who makes everything holy and whole, make you holy and whole, put you together – spirit, soul, and body – and keep you fit for the coming of our Master, Jesus Christ. The One who called you is completely dependable. If he said it, he'll do it!
> *(The Message)*

God wants to fix our fragmented parts. Wherever we have been fractured in spirit, soul, or body, He wants to make us whole. Of course, complete healing and wholeness will not come until our resurrection when Jesus returns and our bodies are transformed to become glorious bodies – yet that process of transformation has already begun to a degree. God is concerned with the whole person and He has a plan for our whole being. We see this reflected in the ministry of Jesus.

A paralysed soul

In Luke 5:17–25 we read the story of a paralysed man whose four friends brought him to Jesus' feet. The house was so crowded where Jesus was that the man's friends took the drastic measure of tearing up the roofing of the house and winching the stretcher down before the Lord. Through the presence of Jesus, the healing power of God was palpable in the house. Luke records that having witnessed this bizarre escapade, Jesus 'saw' the men's faith. It's amazing to think that faith can be seen. Of course, James teaches us that 'faith without works is dead' (James 2:20). It is intriguing to note Jesus' further remarks to the paralysed man. He saw the friend's faith, but He said to the paralysed man:

Man, your sins are forgiven you.

Luke 5:20

Apart from the astounding revelation that Jesus could forgive sins (a claim which the Pharisees were appalled at), this response raises some other questions for us. As far as we know, this paralysed man was not seeking forgiveness of sins but the healing of the body. Of course, it is possible that the Lord, with supernatural knowledge, discerned that the man wanted forgiveness, even though he didn't express this. Or could it actually be that the man needed forgiveness to effect his physical healing? In no way am I suggesting that physical illness is always caused by our personal sins, but sometimes it may be. Certainly, some people can become debilitated physically because they are somehow inhibited spiritually. It is impossible to be certain with this man, but could it be that he needed this release of forgiveness on the inside to effect his healing on the outside? Certainly, we can be sure that there are many people who have been disabled in some way (perhaps not physically speaking) because of wounds of the heart. Perhaps they are crippled by some past memory or immobilised by a paralysing fear?

A woman shamed and shunned

In Luke 8:43–47 we read of the healing of the woman with a haemorrhage. Of course, this was a very personal and embarrassing problem for her, but in the religious culture of the day her complaint also made her ceremonially unclean. In fact, her coming into contact with other people could potentially make them unclean also. In a crowd like this, she was effectively a contaminant. She had tried all the medicines and quack remedies available in her day. All her savings were gone, and despite all her attempts to better her situation, she only grew worse. Have you ever been in such a desperate place as she was? She should not have been in the crowd that day, but she was there in order to touch the hem of Jesus' garment, believing that by doing so she could be healed. Many brushed past Jesus that day, but only one pressed in close to Him by faith. We read that the moment she touched the hem of Jesus' clothing her bleeding stopped.

Potentially that could have been the end of the story: the woman gets healed secretly, and jubilantly sneaks home in the crowd; but that wouldn't do for Jesus. He called the woman out. When she realised that her cover was blown, in fear and trepidation she threw herself at Jesus' feet and told all that had transpired. Why did Jesus do this? Could He not just have left things alone and let the woman get her healing by stealth, rather than subjecting her to such a degree of exposure and embarrassment? Well, Jesus is not in the habit of embarrassing people or needlessly drawing attention to vulnerable people. Indeed, in the case of the healing of the deaf and dumb man (Mark 7:32ff), rather than making a spectacle out of the man's miracle, Jesus 'took him aside, away from the crowd' (Mark 7:33, NIV UK 2011). There had to be a good reason why Jesus drew this woman out into the open.

I believe the reason Jesus did this is indicated in His words to the woman in verse 48:

Daughter, be of good cheer; your faith has made you well. Go in peace.

This lady had been cut off from society and her religious community because of her condition. She had suffered rejection on many levels. For all we know, she may have been divorced by her husband because of it. She certainly was made to feel dirty and shunned. Notice how Jesus addresses her: 'Daughter'. Why does He call her daughter? He is addressing her as a daughter of faith, a daughter of Abraham – meaning 'you belong to God's people'. In other words, by Jesus calling her out from hiding and addressing her in this way, He was effectively saying, 'You're no longer forsaken, but you're part of the family now!' Jesus was receiving her back into the community. Jesus is interested in *all* our needs. It wasn't enough for Jesus that this woman be healed (many of us would have settled for this), He had to restore her integrity as a member of the community. He wanted to heal her rejection as well as her haemorrhage.

Touching the untouchable

A further example of Jesus' compassion for the whole person is seen again in Matthew 8:2-3:

> And behold, a leper came and worshipped Him, saying, 'Lord, if You are willing, You can make me clean.' Then Jesus put out His hand and touched him, saying, 'I am willing; be cleansed.' Immediately his leprosy was cleansed.

Not only do we see Jesus' unquestionable willingness to heal this leper, but we see His tender compassion in how He approached him. What must this man's rejection have been like? In a similar way to the woman with the haemorrhage, the leper was unclean – but, unlike her, he could not hide his condition. It would have been necessary for him to separate himself from society and warn off anyone who came near him by ringing a bell and crying, 'Unclean! Unclean!' We can never know for sure, but was this man ever married? When was the last time he received a kiss of affection? Did he have any children? When did they last jump up on his lap and embrace him? Whatever his relational circumstances were, it is certain that this man would not have received anyone's touch in a very long time. However, as he feels confidence to approach Jesus and submit to Him as 'Lord' (verse 2), Jesus responds by reaching out and touching him. One touch dispels the rejection of many years!

No airbrushing in the Bible

The Bible is not a book filled with fantastic super-heroes, but rather it recounts the very earthy experiences of ordinary, broken people. Even those whom we might class as biblical heroes are portrayed 'warts and all'. In the Bible, human foibles and frailties are not airbrushed out, simply because the whole plotline is leading us to a Saviour who will rescue us from sin and the worst in ourselves.

How wonderful that Jesus is 'willing' to make us whole, as the leper discovered. The difference between the message of the Bible and other religious systems is that we have a Saviour who can deal with our sin and brokenness, because He took it upon Himself on the cross. He took it all upon Himself, as if it were His own, so that we might be healed and set free.

A bruised Saviour for a broken race

In the next chapter, we will begin to look at some of the practical steps we can take in order to receive Christ's healing for our wounds – but before moving on, consider what Jesus did for you on the cross and ponder these immortal words:

He was despised and rejected by men,
A Man of sorrows and acquainted with grief.
And we hid, as it were, our faces from Him;
He was despised, and we did not esteem Him.
Surely He has borne our griefs
And carried our sorrows;
Yet we esteemed Him stricken,
Smitten of God, and afflicted.
But He was wounded for our transgressions,
He was bruised (*crushed*, NIV) for our iniquities;
The chastisement for our peace was upon Him,
And by His stripes we are healed.

Isaiah 53:3–5

A Prayer

Father, I thank You that You sent Your Son, Jesus Christ into this world to rescue me from my sin, my selfishness and my brokenness.

I thank You that because You and Jesus love me so much, He died on the cross bearing all my fallenness. Now I choose to believe that because He was crushed on that cross, by His wounds I can be made perfectly whole.

As I come now to consider some stepping stones to healing, I ask that the sacred medicine that flows from the wounds of Jesus would reach and heal me. Amen.

CHAPTER TEN
THE FOUNDATION OF FORGIVENESS

———•———

It is important not to fall into the trap of seeking some 'formula' that will instantly 'fix' all our problems. Remember, in this life we will always have problems; only in heaven will we have the ultimate solution to everything. Even in these areas of wounding, we must be prepared for a *process* of healing, which often spans many years. In a sense, all of us will be undergoing healing for our whole lifetime! The process of healing incorporates several contributing factors, such as active discipleship and a personal pursuit of God. We must not make the mistake of requiring the healing available from God, but withholding our lives from His Lordship.

The stepping stones to healing in this and the next chapter must not be viewed as a 'formula', but rather as biblical principles that will position us to receive the healing Jesus has purchased for us on the cross. Undoubtedly, forgiveness must be considered the foundation of the healing process rather than a mere stepping stone. Forgiveness with God, through a personal relationship with Jesus Christ as our Saviour and Lord, and an ongoing attitude of forgiveness towards others who offend us, is foundational to a relationship with God.

Jesus taught us to forgive

The subject of forgiveness is one of the most misunderstood worldwide – and the Church is definitely no exception to this. Yet, why is the Church confused about the subject, when it was Jesus who gave us the ultimate and authoritative teaching on the matter? In the Sermon on the Mount, He taught: if you forgive, then you will know the blessings of God's forgiveness flowing to you. When teaching His disciples to pray, He included the element of forgiving one another, Matthew 6:12:

> And forgive us our debts,
> As we forgive our debtors.

Jesus repeats this point immediately after the 'Amen'. Matthew 6:14–15:

> For if you forgive men their trespasses, your heavenly Father will also forgive you. But if you do not forgive men their trespasses, neither will your Father forgive your trespasses.

Obviously the disciples wanted their sins forgiven – who in their right mind wouldn't? However, reading between the lines in the Gospels, it appears the Twelve may have had a struggle forgiving each other.

In Matthew 18:21–22, the ever-vocal Peter asked Jesus how many times he ought to forgive someone an offence. When asking,

Peter offered a figure that he considered more than adequate, indeed, superabundant! 'Seven times?' Actually, Peter *was* being very generous when we consider that the accepted wisdom in rabbinical teaching of the day was to forgive a maximum of three times, but four was thought to be unacceptable. So Peter's estimate was more than double the rabbis'; but not enough for Jesus. Jesus' response to Peter was forgive 'up to seventy times seven' – 490 times! I imagine that the number seven here, which is the biblical number representing perfection and completeness, is indicating that we must offer perfect, complete forgiveness to others. It could never mean that at offence number 491 you could take vengeance on your offender. Surely what Jesus is teaching is: keep on forgiving; stop counting, forgive and forgive and forgive again! This would be particularly relevant for those who have offenders in their lives whom they can't escape, but who perpetuate the offence.

Jesus went on to illustrate to Peter and the other disciples the grave consequences of unforgiveness by telling the Parable of the Unforgiving Servant in Matthew 18:23–35. He told of a servant who the king forgave of a huge debt, today the equivalent to a fortune. Yet this same servant refused to write off a debt owed by his neighbour of a very small amount. The king heard about this and threw the first servant into prison until he could repay the entire amount. Jesus' conclusion to this parable is striking in verses 34–35:

And his master was angry, and delivered him to the torturers until he should pay all that was due to him. So My heavenly Father also will do to you if each of you, from his heart, does not forgive his brother his trespasses.

What does this mean? Well, on a basic level, it certainly teaches that if we harbour bitterness or resentment towards someone, we will not enjoy the benefits and freedom of God's forgiveness. To be more specific, it appears that if we are unforgiving, there is the potential that somehow we will be imprisoned by our bitterness and even overtaken by these 'torturers' that Jesus speaks of. Many believe that these 'torturers' are demonic beings that are given 'rights' to torment us when we harbour resentment in our hearts. Certainly, it is the case that some of the most tormented souls are those who cannot or will not forgive. As we shall see when we consider the demonic realm in the third section of this book, demons are always looking for entry points and 'legal rights' to afflict us. One of the most common 'rights' that demons exploit is unforgiveness in our hearts. Isn't it incredible to think that our wrong reactions to our offenders can do as much harm to us, and even more, than their original offence? The damage unforgiveness does cannot be underestimated; it will imprison and torture us.

So, the Lord Jesus has established a kingdom principle for us in His teaching about forgiveness. If we want to know the continuous blessing of God upon our lives, we need to be continually forgiving others. If we won't forgive our debtors, but then request God to forgive us, we are guilty of rank hypocrisy. We are asking God to do something for us that we are not prepared to do for others. This is how we are captured in a prison of bitterness, a place where the 'torturers' will have their tormenting way with us.

Paul, following on from Jesus' teaching on the 'tormenters', tells us in 2 Corinthians 2:10–11 that when we accommodate unforgiveness in our hearts, Satan can 'take advantage of us'.

I have forgiven that one for your sakes in the presence of Christ, lest Satan should take advantage of us; for we are not ignorant of his devices.

2 Corinthians 2:10–11

The phrase 'take advantage' has been variously translated: 'outwit' (NIV), 'outsmart' (NLT), 'exploit' (NET), giving us the strong impression that one of the most potent schemes of the enemy is to overtake us or overreach us through unforgiveness.

I devote more space to considering the foundation stone of forgiveness compared to the other stepping stones to healing, because it is so fundamental to the process. Where wounds inflicted by others are concerned, forgiveness is often essential to receiving relief and release. Perhaps, while reading the previous chapters on wounds, you have realised the complicity of others in your hurt. The easiest thing to do next is to sit in judgement and direct blame towards them. We might even feel we are 'within our rights' and 'entitled' to feel this way. There is no doubt that all of us possess a God-given sense of justice. However, the problem is that none of us – apart from God – has what it takes to be judge and administrator of true justice. Perhaps, up to this point, your main focus has been on the wounds that *others* have inflicted upon you as the sole cause of your problems. Would you now consider the possibility that your own unforgiveness towards those who hurt you is significantly contributing to your pain and bondage?

The house that pain built

Peter Horrobin, in his excellent book *Forgiveness – God's Master Key*,[1] likens each of our lives to a building with many rooms. Each room contains memories of important events in our lives.

Some of the doors to those rooms are wide open all the time and we happily enjoy the memories they contain. However, some of the doors are closed and locked because there is pain associated with these memories. Some of the closed rooms are named *trauma, rejection, betrayal, abuse, disloyalty, divorce, accidents* and *mistakes*. We have locked these rooms because we don't know how to resolve those painful memories. However, as the years go by, it gets more difficult to cover up the hurt inside us. Some people have so many locked rooms in their lives that they have very little living space left! Often what happens is, the mess on the inside seeps out from under the locked doors. We try to cover it up and carry on as if nothing is happening, but everyone can see the mess. Perhaps, deep down, we know that the only way the mess can be cleared up is to open the door and go inside. The problem is, the key has been thrown away. Peter Horrobin explains that Jesus has given us the master key of forgiveness and He wants us to use it. When we use it, Jesus will then come with us into those rooms and help us clean up the mess.

Maybe you have been experiencing the mess 'seeping' beneath the closed doors of your life. So far in your life you have been an expert in hiding the mess, but now you can't hold it together any more and others are beginning to notice that something is wrong. For some of you, it's not so much the 'seeping' under the doors that betray your woundedness, but there are actually cracks starting to show on the very building of your life!

The choice to forgive

Forgiveness is not a feeling, it is an act of the will. If we wait until we *feel* like forgiving, we will never do it. I would go as far as to suggest that if you feel like forgiving, there probably wasn't much of an offence to forgive in the first place. Forgiveness presupposes that a deep hurt has been inflicted, and the natural response to deep pain is not forgiveness. Don't think that you must get your feelings in order before you can forgive. You can choose to forgive against the grain of every emotion in your being. Corrie ten Boom and her sister Betsie were imprisoned in Ravensbrück concentration camp for rescuing over 800 Jews from the Nazis in World War Two. Her father and her sister Betsie died as a result of being imprisoned by the Nazis. Corrie, having experienced and witnessed some of the worst atrocities of the twentieth century, testifies that in Ravensbrück she learned that forgiveness was an act of the will which could function apart from the heart.

For every Christian, the choice to forgive will be greatly influenced by God's graciously indulgent forgiveness for *our* offences against Him. Yes, to enjoy the benefits of God's forgiveness we must forgive others, but equally, to truly forgive others we must have some heart knowledge of God's lavish forgiveness of our sins. This is why Paul said in Ephesians 4:31–32:

Let all bitterness, wrath, anger, clamour, and evil speaking be put away from you, with all malice. And be kind to one another, tenderhearted, forgiving one another, even as God in Christ forgave you.

In keeping with this revelation, in the most horrendous of circumstances, Corrie ten Boom also said that no pit was so deep that the love of God was deeper still, and that God would supply the love needed to enable us to forgive our enemies. Such statements mean so much more when they come from someone like Corrie ten Boom, who had many enemies who inflicted unspeakable crimes on her and her family. Her experience of the love of God in her own heart eventually enabled her to forgive what, to most, was unforgivable.

'Forgiving yourself'

Of course, the term 'forgiving yourself' is thought by some to be a nonsense statement, because only God can forgive our sins. However, we often use this term to describe how we relate to ourselves concerning the mistakes in our past. Even those who have received God's forgiveness through Jesus often have a hard time accepting that their sins are actually gone and they are accepted by God. Then there are others who do accept this truth, but they can't accept *themselves* for what they have done. God might forgive them, but they won't forgive themselves. Their attitude is: 'Even if God has forgiven me, I feel I don't deserve it, so I'm not going to release myself to enjoy His forgiveness.' They hold themselves under a standard of justice, rather than grace. The devil loves this kind of spiritual territory because it is fertile for him to reproduce more condemnation, guilt and shame.

I will never forget one of the first people I led through the prayer of forgiveness. They knew they needed to forgive several people, but when we came to pray, there was an obvious block. They just couldn't get the words out. I assumed there was something demonic preventing them (and there was deliverance that later took place), but all became clear when they looked up at me and exclaimed: 'How can I forgive these people when I don't even forgive myself?' It turned out that there was a past secret in their life which they had confessed to God and knew they had been forgiven for, but yet they had never forgiven themselves.

Have you been punishing yourself for wrong choices you have made? Are you still carrying guilt and shame for sins God has already forgiven you for? Do you think you don't deserve forgiveness?

Get your list ready!

Most of us have a list of people who have offended us in some way or another. Certainly, all of us have been hurt to the extent that we need to forgive. But before you pray down your list, perhaps – as we have just discussed – you need to put *yourself* at the top of the list of people to forgive. Will you, once and for all, release yourself into the freedom of God's forgiveness, so that you can personally experience it in its fullness and then be able to offer it to others?

Another person who may need to be on your list is God. What!? How could God possibly need our forgiveness? Well, obviously He doesn't need to be forgiven because He has never done anything wrong, let alone anything to hurt or harm us. However, sometimes in life we perceive that God has either directly or indirectly hindered us through things we believe He has done against us, or at least allowed to take place in our lives. Or, perhaps, at times it seemed God did not do what we needed Him to do: He didn't come through for us; He didn't appear to honour His promises or answer our prayers.

We don't have either the space or, frankly, all the answers we need to discuss the problem of evil and suffering which exists in our world. There are many mysteries in life, and I don't pretend to have the answers to them. However, what we can categorically state is that the revelation of God in Jesus Christ, His Son, shows Him to be *good*. He does not seek to harm or hinder us. On the contrary, He has unmistakeably demonstrated His love for us in the death of Jesus on the cross. Yes, because of Adam and Eve's original sin we live in a fallen world where 'stuff' happens: pain, cruelty, betrayal, abuse, disease, war, disaster etc. The blame for that should not be laid at God's feet. Also, God has irrevocably given us free choice, which has consequences not only for us, but for everyone we relate to. Our decisions affect not only ourselves, but others – whether for good or ill. Then we must factor in the enemy of our souls and his network of demons who seek to destroy us. These are all ingredients making up the chaos that can be this life, and yet God so often gets the blame for everything calamitous that happens in our lives and in this world.

Do you need to confess to God any bitterness or resentment towards Him that has been hindering you moving on into healing and freedom? Whilst, for some, 'yourself' might be at the top of the list of those you need to forgive, for others 'thoughts against God' might need to feature with some priority.

For many people, their parents will be first on the list. As we have already discussed, in our development, our parents are the most important people in our lives. We must thank God for good parenting, but we need to forgive parents and other family members for anything said or done that has had a negative impact on our lives.

Others on your list might be your spouse or an ex-partner, your children, a friend or bully, a teacher, a boss, or even a church leader.

Forgiveness or reconciliation?

'But they don't deserve it,' some will object. Others will protest, 'They still persist in the same behaviour.' Then there will be those who feel they cannot forgive a person because they are already dead! Please note something crucial: forgiveness may be part of the journey to reconciliation, but it is not the same thing. People often confuse the two. I remember praying with a young woman who had been abused by a close family member. Previously, when she heard her pastor exhort the congregation to forgive, she got the impression she needed to invite that abuser round to her house for a cup of tea and smooth things out with them! Obviously this thought horrified her, as it should. She would have put herself in a very vulnerable position, potentially exposing herself to further abuse. In various scenarios reconciliation is not possible, but forgiveness is. In the context of healing, you are forgiving an offender primarily for your sake rather than theirs. Until you forgive, it can be as if that offender still has a hold on you in some way. You may still be captive to the memory and chained to the past. Even when reconciliation is impossible or inappropriate, forgiveness needs to take place in order for you to be totally free.

Some Christians take issue with this understanding of 'one-way forgiveness': the concept that we can forgive another whenever we have not been reconciled to them, or even when they have not repented of their deeds. Many Christians believe we should only forgive when a person is remorseful and asks for forgiveness. I believe such a misunderstanding is due to confusing our personal and independent forgiveness of another in order to preserve a healthy relationship with God and ourselves, with reconciliation that restores a healthy relationship with another. Certainly, Jesus taught us we *must* forgive when people repent (Luke 17:4), even seven times in one day, but Jesus was definitely not prohibiting forgiveness when such repentance is not there. Jesus encourages us to reconcile where possible, but if we can't reconcile we must still forgive.

From a gospel perspective, we as sinners come to enjoy the blessings of forgiveness when we repent and believe the Good News. Our forgiveness has already been purchased by Jesus on the cross and it is now offered freely to all in the invitation of the gospel message. Already, God has been reconciled to us through the death of Jesus, but we are now called upon to be reconciled to

God in repentance (2 Corinthians 5:18–20). We, likewise, are to offer our forgiveness to others, even when they have not entered into the goodness of reconciliation with us through saying 'Sorry'.

Jesus, our example

Surely the example of our Lord in His death shows us how we are to behave when wounded by others. Luke 23:34:

> Father, forgive them, for they do not know what they are doing.
>
> *(NIV UK 2011)*

Though those crucifying Jesus that day ignorantly slew the Son of God and showed no remorse in doing so, Jesus was still able to extend forgiveness to them. I want to suggest that Jesus, though He was always putting others before Himself (and especially so on the cross), forgave His offenders in order to keep His heart right before His Father in heaven. When Jesus forgave those who crucified Him, plainly it did not mean that they were, in that moment, forgiven of all their sins and would end up in heaven one day. Some of the soldiers and people in the crowd that day would later repent and believe, but many did not. So what was Jesus doing when He prayed for their forgiveness? I believe that as a Man being wronged by His fellow man, rather than allowing bitterness or resentment to grip His heart, He forgave them and entrusted justice to the only true Judge, God. Is this not what Peter means when he writes in 1 Peter 2:23–24:

> When they hurled their insults at him, he did not retaliate; when he suffered, he made no threats. Instead, he entrusted himself to him who judges justly. 'He himself bore our

sins' in his own body on the cross, so that we might die to sins and live for righteousness; 'by his wounds you have been healed.'

(NIV UK 2011)

Some might exclaim, 'Where is the justice in just forgiving someone who shows no remorse?' The answer is: the justice is where it should be, with God, not with us. We cannot dispense perfect justice. Of course, we are speaking here of personal matters of the heart rather than issues relating to the law of the land. God has ordained the judicial systems of society and the need for punishment (Romans 13:4). Criminal offenders ought to be punished for their deeds, but even when that must take place legally, we can still forgive an offender from our hearts. Here is an important point: when we forgive a person, they are not getting away with it or being let off. On the contrary, think of it like this: we are taking them off our hook and placing them onto God's – the true Judge of all the earth who will ultimately do justly (Genesis 18:25).

Some people will painfully protest: 'But you don't understand, you don't know what they have done to me!' No, I don't, nor do I claim to appreciate what you have endured; but while I don't understand, Jesus does, and He has endured more wrong and suffering than any human being. It is His example that will pave the way to our healing. Paul teaches us how we must approach wrongdoing against us in Romans 12:19:

Do not take revenge … but leave room for God's wrath, for it is written: 'It is mine to avenge; I will repay,' says the Lord.

(NIV UK 2011)

We are to 'leave room for God's wrath' by getting out of the way. We need to stop trying to be judge and let God do His job.

Often, we have no choice but to live with some of the consequences of other people's sins against us. I do not mean that we should be careless about our own welfare or that of others under our care. However, whether we like it or not, we do have to live with the ramifications of what others do against us. The question is: will we live in the bondage of our bitterness, or in the freedom of forgiveness? Jesus shows us that no one genuinely forgives without bearing suffering and pain inflicted by others. What really matters is what we do with that suffering and pain.

Forget about 'Forgive and forget'!

'Forgive and forget' is such a nonsense statement! How can we forget deep pain and tragic memories? What is regrettable, to say the least, is that many erroneously think that if they haven't forgotten, they haven't forgiven. Some of our greatest problems when dealing with wounds come from our attempts to bury the pain or live in denial of it. It *is* total denial to try to forgive and forget. Even God doesn't forget the past – of course, He chooses not to remember our sins (Hebrews 8:12). He keeps no record of our wrongs because He *is* love (1 Corinthians 13:5). He chooses not to recall our sins, but He hasn't developed selective amnesia regarding our millennia of human rebellion. God doesn't change our past of sinfulness or woundedness, but He does redeem and heal it. In order for that to happen, we must no longer be in denial about our pain or seek to erase the troublesome memories, but rather, be honest before Him and face the pain with Him.

The life-changing power of forgiveness

Recently, I prayed with a woman who had a recurring demonic

problem whenever she entered into deep intercessory prayer for the needs of others. She had previously received much healing and deliverance, but a persistent problem remained and would erupt disturbingly when she prayed in this way. As we prayed for her, we wrestled with this demonic force with little progress. After a while of not knowing what to do, a thought came to my mind that I should ask her if there was anyone she needed to forgive. I resisted this thought for a while and persisted in wrestling with the demon. However, the thought kept recurring, so I gave in and asked her. She shared that an old wound had been reopened that very week, simply by reading the name of a person who had hurt her deeply a number of years ago. All the old feelings of injustice, deep anger and even hatred had returned.

I briefly shared with her about the need for her to forgive. She knew it would be hard, but she was prepared to do this. It was obvious as she prayed that her pain and distress over this incident ran very deep. She openly expressed the anger and the betrayal she felt because of this offender. Eventually, she broke down in tears – not because of what the person had done, but because she realised her own bitterness towards them. After she had prayed, I was now ready to take on this strong demonic spirit that had been demonstrating its great influence in her life. So, I then began addressing it and commanding it to go. Before, when addressing this spirit, there had been all sorts of uncomfortable manifestations in this woman's body – but now there was nothing! I mean, *absolutely* nothing! I was expecting at least something of a tussle before the demon left (which, I have found, is often the case), but it appeared that through the simple act of heartfelt forgiveness, this ugly power in her life had completely gone without so much as a squeak! If ever I have witnessed a demonstration of the incredible power of forgiveness, and how the enemy clings to it as a 'right' to afflict us, it was that night. This woman is now completely free and she can pray deeply in intercession without any effect from the enemy. However, she is also keenly aware of the danger of judging others and is careful to keep forgiving others who hurt her.

Do not underestimate the power of forgiveness to set you free from what may even be a lifetime of bondage. A few days ago, I read the story of a minister who had just finished preaching on forgiveness within the Lord's Prayer. It was Communion Sunday and they traditionally included a time of sharing with the Lord's Supper. He had just asked if anyone had something to share, when one of his deacons, an eighty-seven-year-old man, stood up. He began, 'For eighty-four years...' His wife grabbed her mouth with her hand and clenched closed her eyes in praise. 'For eighty-four years I have hated a little boy. Eighty-four years ago this little boy came riding up to me on his bike and said, "Ha, ha, ha, ha, your mother is dead." And this is how I learned my mother had died. Today I want to forgive that boy.' No one in the congregation moved. Breathing almost stopped. Tears broke loose. The only response that the minister could utter was, 'This is a holy moment.' Another person stood up and forgave someone else and then another did the same.[2]

Surrender your pain

If we wait until we feel like forgiving we never will. Forgiveness is not dependent on our emotions, but upon the will. Hopefully, the emotions will eventually come, but you must first *choose* to forgive. Whilst the initial step of forgiving someone may begin with raw, naked volition, it is vital that, if and when emotions do start to rise, you don't suppress them, as this will hinder your healing. The Lord needs to get to our wounds in order to heal them. Often, we block Him reaching inside to our broken parts because, whenever they rise to the surface, we push them down again. Often the motive behind our suppression of emotions is the fear that we'll lose composure, or even control. This is where we must trust the Lord that He won't allow things to become worse, but better long-term. Things may appear to get worse, and certainly pain will feel more acute when you are facing it rather than ignoring it, but that will be short term pain for long-term gain.

Will you allow God's Spirit to bring those painful memories to the surface? Will you honestly acknowledge your shame, fear, anger or whatever else you are feeling towards those who have hurt you? Will you take the hand of Jesus now, go into those closed-off rooms of your past, and allow Him to set you free with the master key of forgiveness? Forgiveness is the foundation on which your healing will rest: forgiveness *from* God and forgiveness *towards* others.

If you feel ready to pray the following prayer, don't pray 'Lord, I want to forgive' or 'God, please help me to forgive'. Exercise your will and pray, 'Lord, I choose to forgive.' It is also preferable that you pray this prayer audibly.

A Prayer

Father, I thank You for Your forgiveness which Jesus purchased for me at the cross. I fully embrace it by faith and choose to release myself into the freedom of Your forgiveness.

I confess holding myself in judgement over my past sins and mistakes, whenever You have declared me completely forgiven. Please release me from all false guilt and shame, and all the condemnation of the devil.

Father, I am sorry for blaming You for anything bad that has happened in my life; for the times I thought You had let me down. I don't understand the difficult things that have happened in my life and the lives of those I love, and perhaps I never will, but I choose to trust You, and believe that You love me more than I could ever imagine. I declare that You would never, ever want to harm me. Please forgive me for any resentment or bitterness towards You and set me free from the consequences of this attitude towards You.

Father, as You have forgiven me in Christ, by an act of my will, I freely choose to forgive all who have ever harmed or wronged me. Especially I forgive *(name them)*, for *(what they did or failed to do)*, which made me feel *(express your emotions without reservation to God)*. I release to You any sense of entitlement to revenge and I let go of all my bitterness and resentment. I ask You to heal my damaged emotions and set me free from any way the enemy has kept me in bondage through unforgiveness. Also, I ask You to bless these people whom I have forgiven. In Jesus' Name I pray. Amen.

———◆———

1. Peter Horrobin, *Forgiveness – God's Master Key* (Lancaster: Sovereign World, 2008).

2. crossrhythms.co.uk/articles/lifefiles/Paul_Nixon/A_Simple_Lesson/13817/p1/ (accessed 14.7.17).

The foundation of forgiveness is indispensable for our healing, but there is more we can do to position ourselves to receive the healing available in the gospel of Jesus Christ. In this chapter, we will briefly discuss some biblical principles which form further stepping stones to our healing.

Repent of ungodly responses to wounding

When we are hurt, we naturally tend to focus our attention on those who have hurt us. Like the proverbial wounded animal, our immediate reaction is to lash out against all potential assailants. If we are serious about being healed from our wounds and being released from any bondage in which the enemy has us, we must face our own failings, particularly in relation to how we have responded to our hurt.

Many people's attitude when offended is: 'You hurt me, I hate you and I'm going to hurt you back!' Others who have been rejected might reason, even subconsciously: 'I'll reject you before you reject me!' Certainly, these responses would explain why, at times, we may find some people somewhat 'prickly'. We might call this 'the hedgehog syndrome': like a hedgehog, whenever we feel threatened, we curl up into a ball and protrude very sharp edges towards others. Often where there has been rejection there is also the *fear* of rejection. We fear having to experience the pain of rejection again, so we shun close relationships lest it happen. Distrust and defensiveness can even begin to invade our existing relationships. We begin to hurt and reject others in the same manner we have been treated. The adage is true: 'hurt people, *hurt* people'.

Self-rejection can also accompany fear of rejection. Low self-esteem can cause a person to conclude, 'I mustn't be likeable, or worth anyone's friendship.' Such a person will probably withdraw from relationships and isolate themselves. This can be a vicious circle, almost a self-fulfilling prophecy, as we bemoan having no friends but simultaneously send out vibes that we are not welcoming any. Proverbs 18:24 offers good advice on how to get friends and keep them:

A man that hath friends must shew himself friendly ...

(KJV)

Many times, I have heard people say, 'Our church is such an unfriendly place' or 'No one ever bothers with me'. No doubt we all need to do much better in befriending others, especially in our church fellowships where we are meant to be bringing the healing of the gospel to the broken. However, I have found that often those who complain about unfriendliness are the last to arrive at church and the first to leave. Whenever there are social opportunities for people to come together to get to know one another better, they don't participate. Rather than it being the case that people do not bother with them, often it is more likely that they *fear* rejection and, as a result, protect themselves from the possibility of it happening by withdrawing from people. This attitude, which the person is often oblivious to, sends out signals to others: 'I want to keep myself to myself – stay away!'

We need to repent of all our wrong attitudes and responses that have developed out of our personal pain. We must take ownership of the ways we have inflicted hurt on others.

Another very real ungodly response is to say: 'I hurt, so I will fix myself my way!' When responding to pain like this, it is likely that control will be a dominating force in your life because, rather than giving control to God, you are taking control yourself. People may try to rescue themselves through living for family, education, career, or sport. However, whilst creating a momentary distraction, these can never solve their deep heart problem. Even if there is a moral or religious veneer to such control, DIY solutions will never work where healing of the heart is concerned.

Give your anger permission

Whilst we should not hurt others out of our personal pain, neither should we compound our personal hurt by denying or suppressing our emotions. Generally, we tend to deal with our pain in either of two extremes: we either externalise it, by hurting others; or we internalise it, which further compounds our own hurt.

Anger has become a taboo; a dirty word to many, especially Christians. We have come to believe it is sinful and prohibited. This attitude has contributed to much false guilt in us for feeling angry and, therefore, the tendency is for us to suppress anger with dangerous consequences. It is a myth that whenever we deny our anger it disappears. Buried anger will either eventually erupt in an unpredictable explosive episode, or it will begin to destroy a person internally, with the potential of even adversely affecting their physical and mental health.

Yes, anger is powerful, but it is not sinful per se. Sex and money are extremely powerful, but they are not inherently wrong; it's how we use them that matters. Equally, with anger, as an emotion it is neutral. The problem comes when we express our anger in destructive ways against others or ourselves. Obviously, this is why Paul said in Ephesians 4:26–27:

'Be angry, and do not sin': do not let the sun go down on your wrath, nor give place to the devil.

Whilst undoubtedly, as Paul says, anger can be expressed sinfully and the devil can get a foothold through it, we can be angry without sinning. In fact, anger expressed healthily without the element of sin is to be encouraged. Therefore, whilst we cannot condone how anger is often exhibited, we must be released from any shame for possessing anger in general. We must give ourselves permission to express it in a manner that will help us in our healing.

God can be angry (Psalm 7:11) and Jesus expressed anger on occasion, particularly against hypocrisy and wickedness (John 2:17); so anger cannot be sinful! We have been created in God's image with emotional response. Emotions were meant to be 'emoted'. Anger, as an emotion, is a bit like a safety valve which is released whenever we are 'letting off steam'. If we don't let the emotion go, it will eventually build up and destructively explode. So, we need to embrace all our emotions, including anger, as originally created by God.

Essentially, anger is a warning, a kind of signal, indicating to us that something deeper is wrong and in need of attention. Anger is a bit like a signal light on a car dashboard telling us something needs mechanical attention. We wouldn't dream of removing the little bulb that's lighting up the board and then convincing ourselves that the problem has disappeared, that would be absurd! Rather, we will take the car to a mechanic in order to get the deeper problem fixed. Anger usually is not *the* problem, but rather the indicator signalling that something deeper is in need of attention.

Anger is often a pointer that there is a sense of injustice deep within us. Something has happened that we deem to be 'just not fair'. Current anger can be rooted in our past, particularly where there have been childhood hurts and unresolved issues. If we have been betrayed, we can become angry because of the breach of trust and loss of confidence. We feel shamed, devalued and confused. Perhaps we may even be angry with ourselves for having been foolishly 'taken in' by someone who took advantage of us. Whenever other people fail to meet our expectations of them, or when we fail to meet our own expectations of ourselves, we can become angry. When our life goals and aspirations are blocked, we can become angry. The potential reasons for our anger are almost endless, but it is vital that we discern the reasons why we are angry.

So, what do we do with our anger? We must learn to express any anger we have, but not in a way that hurts others or ourselves.

How can that possibly be done? Take your anger to God. Of course, He already knows how angry we feel, but the difference in articulating it will be getting it off our chest in the presence of the only One who can truly help us. Whatever it sounds like, we need to honestly unburden our souls before the Lord. This is what the psalmists often did in quite colourful language at times (e.g. Psalms 73, 88). They often began by vehemently complaining about the success of the wicked or the adverse circumstances in their own lives or nation; however, often the tone of these psalms turns to praise, as the angry psalmist gets relief, having been unburdened before God.

Forgiveness is essential, but for forgiveness to be authentic we must be honest with our feelings. God does not require us to be *nice* when speaking to Him, but He does ask us to be *real*. The depth of our hurt must be expressed in honest terms if we want to be released from the power of our pain.

Repent of ungodly substitutes

As we have stated before, the addictive cycle usually begins with pain; pain seeks out pleasure. We seek solace for our suffering in a pleasurable distraction or an artificial high, which will momentarily block our pain. We attempt to fill our inner emptiness with counterfeit satisfactions. Again, it's important to realise that this is why repentance often does not work for some people caught in the habitual spiral of sin. They need healing for the wounds for which the sinful behaviour has become a coping mechanism. Wholeness and true being must fill the void within us.

Through the prophet Jeremiah, God called His people to repentance for having favoured substitute satisfactions over Him – the true source of lasting well-being. Jeremiah 2:13 states:

For My people have committed two evils:
They have forsaken Me, the fountain of living waters,
And hewn themselves cisterns – broken cisterns that can
hold no water.

We must repent of all ungodly substitutes and sinful coping mechanisms getting in the way of our healing and ultimate freedom.

Break ungodly ties

In Chapter Six, we considered the close heart ties that can be established with family, friends, lovers, abusers and all kinds of acquaintances. When these are negative ties, they can compromise us in many ways – not least, by allowing the devil to use these relationships as channels through which he can oppress us. People might reason: 'But those harmful relationships are all in the past.' Though a relationship may be terminated for whatever reason, in a sense, it is not in the past if it is still affecting us in the present.

It is vital that we do what we can to sever these spiritual heart ties and, where possible,[1] remove the influences entirely. These heart ties should be broken through prayer, but it is crucial that a person desires it and does what is practically necessary to sever the spiritual bond. Healthy boundaries may also need to be established.

Allow God to surface your pain

As we have established, emotions should be expressed, preferably at the time we feel them. However, we tend to suppress our emotions with destructive results. Many of us have developed an automatic pattern of denial and suppression when it comes to our feelings. This makes it difficult to get healing, because we are so afraid of facing our pain that we effectively hide it deep within our being. When the Holy Spirit begins to minister to us, He will bring this woundedness to the surface for healing and release. If we go to our default impulse and push it down, burying the pain again, we will not receive the healing.

We must become present to our pain in order to be healed. We must allow the Lord to bring our wounds to the surface. Many of us have within, as it were, a lake of tears covered with a layer of ice. We need to allow the Lord to break through that layer of freezing ice and let the warm tears rise up and out of us. Emotional release is most definitely a part of the process of healing, we must not resist it. Will you give God permission to be Lord of your wounds and hurt?

Allow your wounds to be exposed and permit your pain to come to the surface, so that you can release it to Jesus your Saviour, who absorbed it all on the cross. Let it all come up and out of you and into Him; then let Him fill you with His grace and life.

In the beginning, God's Spirit hovered over the creation and brought order to the chaos. In the New Creation, God's Spirit wishes to 'make all things new' (Revelation 21:5). Will you come to Jesus by faith, so that you may experience the healing you need? God's heart is towards you; God loves you and wants to help you. Peter invites us in 1 Peter 5:7 to:

Give all your worries and cares to God, for he cares about you.

(NLT)

Think of it: with all that is going on in our world and, indeed, in the whole of the universe, *you* are God's great concern, so why don't you choose to trust Him to care for you now?

A Prayer

Lord Jesus, I thank You that You were rejected, forsaken and wounded for me, so that I could be saved and healed.

I confess to You the times when I have reacted in ungodly ways to the offences of others: whether by rejecting others before they rejected me; hurting others or myself by my anger; indulging in sinful practices as a coping mechanism; or turning to other loves for satisfaction. I confess to suppressing my anger and other painful emotions for fear of losing control and, in so doing, preventing You from reaching my scars. I confess any ways in which I have attempted to 'fix' myself, rather than turning to You. I repent of all these sins and I ask Your forgiveness.

Lord Jesus, I ask You now that You would break any ungodly soul tie I have with (*name the people, place, organisation, or object you have been tied to. When persons, these are often the same people that you have forgiven*). Lord, I ask You that all parts of (*be specific in naming*) still tied to me in a wrong way will return to them, and any part of me tied to them wrongly will return to me. Separate me spirit, soul and body from them, and cleanse me from all defilement. Put Your cross between me and all these people.

I choose to become present to my pain in Your presence. I ask that the Holy Spirit would bring my woundedness to the surface so that it may come up and out of me and into You, Lord, for I believe that You bore it all on the cross.

Thank You, Lord Jesus, that by Your wounds I have been healed. I ask You now that Your healing and wholeness will flow from Your wounds to me and fill all my emptiness with Your being and worth. Amen.

———•———

1. Of course, particularly in close family relationships, it is not always possible, nor would it be right, to sever all contacts.

DEMONS

For this purpose the Son of God was manifested, that He might destroy the works of the devil.

1 John 3:8

CHAPTER TWELVE
ANOTHER WORLD

———•———

Sins must be *repented of,* *wounds* need to be *healed,* and *demons* must be *expelled.* A *wound* or *sin* cannot be *cast out,* a *sin* or *demon* cannot be *healed,* and a *demon* or *wound* cannot be *repented of.* It is imperative that we distinguish these barriers to blessing in our lives, so that we can address them with the correct approach.

Already, we have concluded that repentance may not be enough for someone caught in an addictive behaviour when they possess wounds that need healing. Some people use the sinful cycle as a coping mechanism for pain, so in order to overcome this behaviour it is crucial that their wounds are healed. That 'pain seeks out pleasure' is an understanding that many counsellors and rehabilitation groups would acknowledge, but what most of them probably would not recognise is that there can often be demonic empowerment behind certain sinful patterns. Our wilful and habitual sins, when we allow them to go unchallenged and unchecked, have the potential to open up doorways of danger through which the demonic can gain an influence upon us. The enemy loves brokenness and, as we have discovered, from the very beginning of time he has sought to inflict brokenness upon humanity, and exploit its presence in our world and in each of our lives to his advantage. Satan can often use wounds to gain a foothold in our lives. So, what we are saying is: demons can enter our lives through sin and demons can 'infect' our wounds.

A spiritual health warning

When it comes to people's approach to the devil and demons, there are generally two extremes: disbelief and infatuation. Postmodernism, and the Western 'materialist' outlook on life, would lead many in our society to debunk the concept of the demonic realm as mere medieval myth. They reason that now, in our more enlightened age, we can interpret such myths as being representative of the non-personal presence of evil in our world. This perception has even influenced the Church, which in many quarters is inhabited by countless 'practical unbelievers' in the devil and his works. Largely, disbelief in the supernatural has become the established position of the modern West, and this has most certainly been adopted by some significant branches of the Church.

The other extreme is equally undesirable: infatuation and obsession with darkness. Whenever we become practically aware of the existence of the kingdom of darkness, it can breed within us an unhealthy curiosity regarding things 'otherworldly'. Our Lord taught us to pray:

... deliver us from the evil one.

Matthew 6:13

It would seem rather futile to pray for such a reprieve, only then to deliver ourselves over to an obsessive contemplation of darkness.

A number of years ago, I was preaching in Wales on the topic of 'How to Practise the Presence of God'. In the course of my message, I warned against the error of practising the presence of *sin*, practising the presence of *self*, or practising the presence of *Satan*, as opposed to practising God's presence with us and within us. In relation to practising Satan's presence, I relayed how some Christians become so preoccupied with the enemy that they are robbed of their peace in God. Yes, we believe strongly in biblical spiritual warfare – we are told not to be 'ignorant of [Satan's] schemes' (2 Corinthians 2:11, NASB) – but sometimes we can become so engrossed in wrestling with the darkness around us that we get sucked into its wake. We contend with the dark at the expense of switching on the light. The danger is, we begin to see demons everywhere! There *are* a lot of demons around, but they ought never to be our primary focus.

Having shared this truth in that small house fellowship, an elderly lady, who had difficulty walking, called me over to tell me something. She began relating the story of a pastor she had heard about who had planted a church in an extremely evil area. As I recall, even their borrowed meeting place was used by the community for all sorts of ungodly activities during the rest of the week. Whenever the church met on a Sunday morning, the pastor made it his practice to 'bind' all the demonic spirits that he felt had been operating in that place and the local vicinity. I am not, for one moment, suggesting that such an exercise is never warranted. However, the pastor reported that each week it was taking him a longer period of time to get his worship service started properly, as there were more and more spirits to bind. The worship of God was getting pushed back, week on week, as he wrestled with the darkness. Confused by this, he shared the problem with a wise mentor in his life. 'You know what is happening?' the friend said. 'Every demon in the district is coming to your church, because they know they are getting plenty of attention!'

Here is a valuable lesson for us to learn: Satan loves to show off! He craves attention because he needs it to gain a higher profile. So often we gift him with this, by giving him unnecessary air time and publicity.

Some 'deliverance ministries' have become imbalanced in their exclusive concentration on grappling with demons. Not every problem is a demonic one. People can have mental, emotional, physical and even spiritual issues that are not derived from demonic spirits. How distressing it must be for a person, whenever an overzealous but undiscerning 'minister' tries to exorcise a demon that is not there! Sadly, for this and other reasons, there are some vulnerable souls who have come to require deliverance *from* the influence of some unstable 'deliverance ministries'!

So then, we must maintain balance, steering away from these two extremes of disbelief and infatuation. C.S. Lewis, in *The Screwtape Letters*, captured this balance well when he wrote that there were two errors we can fall into: disbelieving in the existence of the demonic realm, or to have an unhealthy and excessive interest in the enemy. Both, said Lewis, delight the forces of hell.[1]

Whenever we do see the enemy evicted from people's lives and great deliverance taking place, we must always maintain our centre of balance, as our Lord exhorted His disciples to in Luke 10:20:

Nevertheless do not rejoice in this, that the spirits are subject to you, but rather rejoice because your names are written in heaven.

An alternative reality

Many of us are oblivious to the spiritual dimension that exists intermingled with the physical. Our creation is inhabited by both celestial and terrestrial beings. Celestial beings are essentially spiritual entities from the angelic and demonic realms.[2] Terrestrial beings are the physical creatures in the natural world. The human being is unique in respect of possessing both terrestrial and celestial attributes. The human being is both physical and spiritual. They are a kind of 'interface' between two worlds; a point of interaction between two alternative realities.

In Genesis 3, we read how Satan entered the Garden of Eden in the form of the serpent, and wrested the dominion of the earth from Adam through deception. Ever since that event, and humanity's subsequent fall into sin, Satan has been manipulating human beings. The Amplified Bible, Classic Edition's translation of Ephesians 2:1–2 graphically depicts Satan's influence upon unbelievers when it says:

You were following the course and fashion of this world [were under the sway of the tendency of this present age], following the prince of the power of the air. [You were obedient to and under the control of] the [demon] spirit that still constantly works in the sons of disobedience [the careless, the rebellious, and the unbelieving, who go against the purposes of God].

Unbelievers are said to be 'under the control of the demon spirit' who works in the children of disobedience. There appears to be no such a thing as neutrality in this world. A person is either under the influence of God, or Satan. Whilst many people may feel they are free and totally independent entities, they do not realise that they are the playground for demonic forces that are pulling their strings. Paul, in 2 Timothy 2:26, relates how some people are in:

> ... the snare of the devil, having been taken captive by him to do his will.

Though we may consider ourselves to be autonomous free will agents, in fact, many of us are manipulated by a dark underworld. We have already observed from the mission statement of the Messiah (Isaiah 61:1) that, among other things, the reason why Jesus came into the world was:

> To proclaim liberty to the captives,
> And the opening of the prison to those who are bound ...

It is precisely because of the demonic enslavement sin and suffering has brought upon us that Jesus came into the world to rescue us. He entered our world to break the fetters of sin and emancipate us from demonic dungeons.

The Deliverer

Jesus Christ came not only to be our Saviour from sin and our Healer of wounds, but He came to be our Deliverer from darkness. Jesus Christ came into this world to undo what sin and Satan has done to our lives. First John 3:8 declares:

The Son of God appeared for this purpose, to destroy the works of the devil.

(NASB)

The Greek word John used which is translated 'destroy', is *luō*: the verb 'to loose'. It can likewise be rendered: 'to dissolve, to sever, to demolish'. The root meaning of *luō* is 'to come unstuck'. So in effect, Jesus our Deliverer came into this world to *dissolve* the network of darkness; to *sever* the grip of wickedness; to *demolish* the superstructure of Satan; and to *dismantle* the strongholds of the devil. He came to 'destroy' the domination of Satan's kingdom in our world. In similar fashion, Hebrews 2:14–15 says:

Inasmuch then as the children have partaken of flesh and blood, He Himself likewise shared in the same, that through death He might destroy him who had the power of death, that is, the devil, and release those who through fear of death were all their lifetime subject to bondage.

Though the English word 'destroy' is used again here in Hebrews, the writer uses a different Greek word, *katargeō*: *kata* meaning 'down' and *argos* meaning 'inactive'. So this word means 'to reduce to inactivity'; 'to render idle, unemployed, inactive, inoperative'. In other words, Jesus our Deliverer came to this planet to put the devil out of business! For each of us on a personal level, Jesus came to free us from every evil and demonic influence.

The sign of the kingdom's advent

When Jesus healed a demonised man who was blind and mute, the Pharisees accused Him of casting out the demon by the power of Beelzebub, the prince of the demons (Matthew 12:22ff). In the course of answering this accusation, Jesus – pointing out how Satan doesn't cast *himself* out – made this important statement recorded in Matthew 12:28:

> But if I cast out demons by the Spirit of God, surely the kingdom of God has come upon you.

Jesus appears to be citing His ministry of delivering the afflicted from demons as a sign that God's kingdom was arriving in their midst. The casting out of demonic spirits was an indicator that the kingdom of God had overtaken them.

The deliverance ministry of Jesus surpassed all Old Testament precedents. In the Old Testament, there *are* examples of demonic activity and some people who were momentarily relieved of oppression,[3] but there is nothing that equates to the casting out of a demon in a New Testament sense. Whilst there are many wonderful miracles and signs in the Old Testament record, there is no account of anyone casting out a demon. Plainly, this would suggest that the casting out of demons was a ministry reserved for the Messiah as a unique demonstration of the arrival of God's kingdom among them. Significantly, when the earthly ministry of Jesus recorded in the Gospels is analysed, it is discovered that around *one-third* of His ministry was that of deliverance!

When Peter came to preach the gospel to the Roman centurion, Cornelius, and his whole household, Peter told them:

> ... how God anointed Jesus of Nazareth with the Holy Spirit and with power, who went about doing good and healing all who were oppressed by the devil, for God was with Him.
>
> *Acts 10:38*

Peter's point clearly mirrors Isaiah 61:1, not least in his emphasis upon Jesus 'healing all who were oppressed by the devil'. Again, it is interesting to note here how deliverance is referred to as an aspect of the ministry of 'healing'. This is in keeping with the plurality of the 'gifts of healings' spoken of in 1 Corinthians 12:9, 28, 30.

The Stronger Man

In Matthew 12:29, Jesus describes, if you will, the operational logistics of defeating Satan, the strong man:

> ... how can one enter a strong man's house and plunder his goods, unless he first binds the strong man? And then he will plunder his house.

Jesus is the Stronger Man who has invaded Satan's house and overcome him. He has dismantled his weaponry and is now claiming his spoils. Our deliverer, Jesus Christ, accomplished this for us through His death on the cross and victorious resurrection from the dead. Often as Christians, we understand the benefits of Jesus' death for us in relation to the forgiveness of our sins, but we fail to appreciate the full ramification of what Christ accomplished for us at Calvary. At the cross Jesus defeated Satan for ever!

> Having disarmed principalities and power, He made a public spectacle of them, triumphing over them in it.
>
> *Colossians 2:15*

The message of the gospel incorporates the defeat of the enemy's influence in all of our lives. However, as we shall explore further,

141

in experience, this victory over sin and the enemy is by no means automatic, nor should it be taken for granted by those who have believed in Christ as Saviour. Many Christians are influenced by the demonic realm in various ways, and they need to know how to personally appropriate the victory of the cross for their lives.

A Prayer

Father, I worship You, not only as the God of all creation, but also as the 'Father of spirits' (Hebrews 12:9).

Forgive me for the times when I have lived as if the material world of time and sense was the only reality. I ask You to open my eyes in a safe way to the spiritual realm, but protect me from being preoccupied with Satan or his ways in an unhealthy manner.

Father, I thank You for the all-encompassing victory over Satan and sin accomplished by Your Son, Jesus, on the cross. I confess Jesus Christ as Lord, and that He is the Stronger Man who has bound Satan and spoiled his goods. Father, I ask You that the power of Christ's victory on the cross would be applied to every area of my life.

If there are any demonic influences in my life, please show me them now and instruct me in Your ways of freedom. In Jesus' Name I pray. Amen.

———•———

1. C.S. Lewis, *The Screwtape Letters*, originally 1942 (London: Harper Collins, 1996).

2. There are various differing kinds of angels and demons in the celestial category.

3. In 1 Samuel 16:23, King Saul was distressed by a tormenting spirit, but found relief whenever David played his harp. However, this was not a deliverance in the New Testament sense.

CHAPTER THIRTEEN
CHRISTIAN IMMUNITY?

Many Christians can accept that *as* Christians we must engage in ongoing repentance for our constant sinful struggles. There is also awareness among some that as Christians we must receive ongoing healing for our wounds, both historic and current. However, the notion that we could have demonic problems as Christians is not only foreign to most professing believers, but to many it is a downright repugnant suggestion!

It is a common belief in much of the Church that the Christian is somewhat immune from serious demonic activity. Especially within evangelicalism and even in some Pentecostal traditions, there has been the concept that if you are born again and Spirit-filled, the demonic could never be afflicting you to any significant degree. Whatever theological discussions might be had around this issue, I would contend that such a position is both logically and practically implausible. Let me explain. I have not yet met a Christian, whether young in the faith or mature, who has claimed that because they are born again or Spirit-filled, sin is no longer a problem for them. None would say that, because Jesus lives in them, the old fallen nature within never ever causes them a problem with ungodly appetites or tendencies towards wrong actions, thoughts or words. Likewise, I have not met a Christian who has claimed that the world no longer causes them a problem with tantalising temptations that like a magnetic draw appeal to their sinful flesh. Yet, I have met many Christians who hold the view that the devil cannot touch them because Jesus lives within them and they are 'under the blood'.

Protection or presumption?

I remember meeting one such professing Christian, who had claimed that he was experiencing spiritual problems after visiting a historical tour of a prison. Without his prior knowledge, the history tour transitioned into a kind of séance in an attempt to contact the ghosts of some of the ancient prisoners. Instead of removing himself from the tour, this man (who professed to be a Christian, but admitted he was not living right before the Lord) decided to stay there on the basis that *because* he was a Christian, he was therefore God's child and under the blood of Jesus.

I began to share with this man the story of the Passover (Exodus 12). On the night the death angel passed through Egypt, slaying the firstborn, the Israelites were instructed to shed a lamb's blood and paint it on the lintels and doorposts of their houses for divine protection. However, their protection was contingent upon them remaining in their house under the shelter of the blood. I pointed out to this man that he had effectively tested the Lord through presumption. The Israelites were only protected when they stayed in their houses, and we must not presume upon God's protection whenever we are co-operating with the enemy. When we are wilfully disobedient, we effectively step out from under God's covering of protection and are exposed to the enemy's attack. Likewise, many Christians today feel the liberty to dabble in sin and darkness and think that it will be without consequence. The attitude is: 'Even if I do sin, "a little talk with Jesus makes it right".' Of course, there is no doubt that the Lord is faithful to forgive us when we sincerely confess our sins (1 John 1:9), but being forgiven does not exclude the possibility of further spiritual repercussions.

In our strong adherence to the doctrine of grace and the forgiveness of sin upon confession, we are in danger of being deluded into believing that there will be no long-term fallout from our disobedience. Doubtless, God has protected us many times when we have been faithless and rebellious; however, God's protection must not be presumed upon when we defy His Word.

It is shocking to discover some of the occult and New Age practices that some Christians wilfully engage in, or the objects that they bring into their homes under the impression that they are neutral and harmless. Isaiah describes God's people in his day as having compromised to an incredible degree with the evil of the unbelieving world around them:

> You, LORD, have abandoned your people, the descendants of Jacob. They are full of superstitions from the East; they practise divination like the Philistines and embrace pagan customs.
>
> *Isaiah 2:6 (NIV UK 2011)*

New Testament warnings

The New Testament in its entirety was written to Christians in the early Church. Even the Gospel records were originally given to the Church. This means that all the scriptural exhortations that warn about the devil and his works are addressed to people who have already come to faith in Christ. There are obvious warnings to Christians not to be ignorant of Satan's schemes (2 Corinthians 2:11) and to be alert to the threat the enemy poses to our lives. There are many examples of such scriptures; here are two significant ones:

> Be sober, be vigilant; because your adversary the devil walks about like a roaring lion, seeking whom he may devour. Resist him, steadfast in the faith ...
>
> *1 Peter 5:8–9*

> For we do not wrestle against flesh and blood, but against principalities, against powers, against the rulers of the darkness of this age, against spiritual hosts of wickedness in the heavenly places. Therefore take up the whole armor of God, that you may be able to withstand in the evil day ...
>
> *Ephesians 6:12–13*

If the devil is no threat to the Christian, these are redundant scriptures. Why would Peter and Paul both exhort us to 'resist' Satan and adorn ourselves in heavenly 'armour' for battle if there is Christian immunity in the spiritual war?

In addition to the above scriptures, there are many more that would indicate the Christian's susceptibility to demonic attack and influence. A strong example of this would be 2 Corinthians 11:3–4:

> But I fear, lest somehow, as the serpent deceived Eve by his craftiness, so your minds may be corrupted from the

simplicity that is in Christ. For if he who comes preaches another Jesus whom we have not preached, or if you receive a different spirit which you have not received, or a different gospel which you have not accepted – you may well put up with it!

Paul is afraid that the serpent (Satan) who deceived Eve at the beginning would also deceive these Corinthian Christians into accepting a counterfeit Jesus, a false gospel – but also note, they were in danger of receiving a 'different spirit' than the Holy Spirit whom they had already received. What does such a statement mean if it is not possible for a Christian with the Holy Spirit to receive another spirit?

Paul warned Timothy that in the last days Christians could be deceived by demons:

Now the Spirit expressly says that in latter times some will depart from the faith, giving heed to deceiving spirits and doctrines of demons ...

1 Timothy 4:1

The Galatians were an example of this, in that they came under the influence of a 'bewitching' spirit which seduced them into believing another gospel (Galatians 3:1).

We know that Satan spoke through Simon Peter, attempting to prevent Jesus going to the cross. Jesus addressed Simon Peter and said:

Get behind Me, Satan! You are an offense to Me ...

Matthew 16:23

A few moments previously, the Father had revealed through Simon Peter's confession that Jesus was the Christ, the Son of the Living God, yet within moments it appears that the devil was able to speak through him.

It is recorded in Acts 5 that some of the first Christians, Ananias and Sapphira, had pretended to give all the proceeds of the sale of their field to the apostles, when in fact they kept back some of the amount for themselves. Peter's rebuke to them insinuates how deep the roots of demonic deception were in their souls:

> But Peter said, 'Ananias, why has Satan filled your heart to lie to the Holy Spirit and keep back part of the price of the land for yourself?
>
> *Acts 5:3*

Obviously, Satan had a staging ground of greed and avarice in these two lives and from that foothold he 'filled' their whole hearts. Herein lies a principle that applies to us all: give Satan a *foothold* and he will seek to make it a *stronghold*, which will eventually become a *stranglehold* that will squeeze the life right out of you. If you give Satan ground in your life, he will claim that area and camp upon it. He will take up residence in your life if you give him a right to be there.

We are in a spiritual war and Satan wants to take us out! Is it not logical that Satan would be more interested in getting us between his crosshairs now that we are Christians, than before, when we were no threat to him? Paul encourages us to be vigilant in battle against these demonic forces that would overtake us, 2 Corinthians 10:3–5:

For though we walk in the flesh, we do not war according to the flesh. For the weapons of our warfare are not carnal but mighty in God for pulling down strongholds, casting down arguments and every high thing that exalts itself against the knowledge of God, bringing every thought into captivity to the obedience of Christ ...

Does this sound like someone immune to the threat of Satan? On the contrary, Paul warns us that Satan can 'take advantage' of us (2 Corinthians 2:11) and we must beware of giving him a 'foothold' (Ephesians 4:27, NIV UK 2011). Like a rock climber who needs only a small crevice or ledge to fix their fingers or toes on to push themselves up, so all Satan needs is a small area of our lives to gain leverage for his agenda against us.

Can a Christian be demon-possessed?

The possibility of a Christian being afflicted by a demonic spirit is often rejected on the grounds of the belief that *a Christian cannot be demon-possessed.* It is the case that most, if not all, English translations of the Bible use the term 'possession' in relation to demonic affliction. However, in our minds the idea of 'possession' usually carries with it the meaning of 'ownership'. We conclude, then, that a Christian could never be 'owned' by the devil, therefore a Christian could never be 'possessed'. The English term 'possession' has also been popularised for us through tradition, folklore and horror genres to convey the most extreme kind of satanic control, which is difficult to conceive of in the life of a child of God. Actually, the word translated 'demon possession' is the Greek word *daimonizomai*, which literally means 'under the power of a demon';[1] there is no sense of ownership or absolute control in this word. Rather, the word in its definition and biblical context connotes the idea of influence. When we think of 'possession', we tend to think of the demoniac of Gadara (Mark 5:1ff) who had a demonic entity called 'Legion' within him. A Roman legion had anywhere between 3,000 to 5,000 soldiers. This certainly implies that this man was heavily controlled by demons. Of course, this is explicit in the Gospel record in Mark 5:3–5:

> ... who had his dwelling among the tombs; and no one could bind him, not even with chains, because he had often been bound with shackles and chains. And the chains had been pulled apart by him, and the shackles broken in pieces; neither could anyone tame him. And always, night and day, he was in the mountains and in the tombs, crying out and cutting himself with stones.

It would appear unthinkable that a Holy Spirit-indwelt Christian could end up in such a state as this poor man. However, in the Gospels the term *daimonizomai* is not reserved in its use for these more extreme examples of massive demonic control, but is also used in reference to those who had severe diseases, either physical or mental, such as paralysis, blindness, deafness, loss of speech, epilepsy, insanity etc.[2] So the term *daimonizomai*, commonly translated 'possession', does not carry the sense of ownership and can refer to much lesser afflictions than the 'Legion' which controlled the demoniac. Demonic 'influence' appears to be the essence of this word.

The sliding scale of demonic influence

When we consider demonic activity in terms of 'influence' rather than ownership, we realise that it's not so much an issue of 'Are we possessed, or are we not?', but rather an issue of how much influence the demonic has upon us, from lesser to greater degrees.

Most Christians are aware that the devil can attack their mind with lying and intrusive thoughts. This is the most common level of influence that Christians experience. Of course, Satan's strategy is that the seed thoughts planted in our minds would be accepted by us and find root in our emotions and eventually our behaviours. It is in this progression that Satan will gain an influence over our lives. So the sliding scale of influence begins with the thoughts the enemy plants in our minds, but may well peak with a heavy influence of demonic control over our behaviour. The extent of the enemy's influence in any life depends upon how much right we have given him to be there. This is fundamental to understanding how Satan gains access to our lives: we can give him the rights to be there. You may own a car, but you can give permission for another person to enter it and drive it. Similarly, Jesus may own your life, but you can allow an enemy force to influence you. Even if you are in the driving seat of your own car, it is possible that there might be some unsavoury backseat drivers who occasionally reach over your shoulder and try to distract or even redirect you!

A simple way to understand the function of a demon is as an empowering force. Just as the Holy Spirit empowers godly choices in obedience to God's Word, so the devil seeks to empower ungodly choices against God's Word. We should think of demonic spirits as the empowering forces behind much driven behaviour. This helps to demystify the demonic realm and it also explains why some people find it so difficult to overcome certain behaviours. We know that the sinful flesh is powerful and very difficult to resist on its own; however, when energised by the demonic, a sinful cycle is very hard to break.

Of course, this is further compounded when the sin is a coping mechanism for a wound.

Some Christians object: 'How can a temple of the Holy Spirit be inhabited by another spirit?' Surely, the same reasoning could be used to argue: 'How can sin remain in the same body and soul as the Holy Spirit?', but evidently it does. There are many other scriptural, theological arguments *for* the assertion that a Christian can receive a demon, but my purpose here is not to formulate a defence of this. However, let it be categorically stated that whilst Scripture is used to argue both *for* and *against* this position, Scripture nowhere disallows such an interpretation.[3]

Is it possible that there might be hidden demonic influences in your life that you are unaware of? Perhaps through your own sinful behaviour or the hurts in your life, the enemy has gained a *foothold*, which became a *stronghold*, which is now a *stranglehold* crushing the life out of you?

In the following chapters, we will consider the practical ways the demonic gains access to our lives. As we explore these, would you agree to prayerfully open your heart so that God would show you any areas where Satan has gained a demonic foothold, which is empowering his purposes in your life?

A Prayer

Father, I thank You that Your Son, the Lord Jesus Christ, defeated Satan at the cross. I ask that His victory would be appropriated to my life.

Forgive me if I have been ignorant of Satan's schemes against me. Forgive me if I have been negligent to fight with the weapons You have given me. Forgive me if I have ever presumed upon Your protection whenever I have co-operated with the enemy.

Please reveal to me any ways that the enemy may have made inroads into my life. Show me the areas where I have given him a right to influence me. Open my mind, and my spiritual eyes and ears, to perceive any demonic influence at work in me, and lead me in Your path of freedom. Amen.

———•———

1. Thayer's Greek Lexicon, *daimonizomai*, www.blueletterbible.org (accessed 14.7.17).

2. Strong's Concordance, Strong's Number G1139 matches for *daimonizomai*, www.blueletterbible.org (accessed 14.7.17).

3. For further balanced research on this matter I would recommend C. Fred Dickason, *Demon Possession and the Christian: A New Perspective* (Chicago, IL: Moody Press, 1987).

CHAPTER FOURTEEN
THE FOOT IN THE DOOR

It appears both reasonable and scriptural that deliverance from demons is a ministry that may be administered both to God's children and to those who will become God's children through the process of ministry. Therefore, it follows that a person may become 'demonised' either before or after their conversion to Christ. The question we will begin to consider in this chapter is: how do these demonic spirits gain access into our lives? What are the entry points commonly used by demons, whereby they get their foot in the door and exercise 'squatters' rights' in certain areas of our lives? 'Squatters' rights' apply whenever someone who does not own a property occupies it long enough to gain certain legal rights to stay. This is similar to how the demonic seeks to achieve admittance into our lives and maintain occupancy by asserting the rights that it has acquired. The treatment of demonic entry points in this chapter will by no means be exhaustive, but it will give a general idea as to how the enemy can secure influence over us.

Knowing participation in sin

Whenever we knowingly and wilfully indulge any sin without confession, repentance, or challenge, we are in serious danger of giving the enemy a foothold in our lives. We have already cited the dangerous delusion that there could be such a thing as inconsequential sin. Even our *forgiven sins* can result in serious practical ramifications, as King David discovered after his adultery with Bathsheba and his subsequent murder of Bathsheba's husband, Uriah. Even though God had blotted out David's sins for ever, after his downfall his family would never be the same again. If the practical ramifications of our sins were not bad enough, our sins can also induce spiritual after-effects allowing the demonic to afflict us. Remember, what the enemy seeks is that 'foothold' (Greek: *topos*, Ephesians 4:27). Like the small ledge or crevice upon which the rock climber seeks to get a grip, Satan the arch-legalist seeks authority to build a stronghold, gaining a chokehold over us.

1. Idolatry

Psalm 96:5 tells us:

> For all the gods of the nations are idols, but the LORD made the heavens.

The first and second of the Ten Commandments forbids the worship of false gods and idols, but what the New Testament further reveals to us is that the demonic is the prime mover behind all false religion and idolatry. Paul says in 1 Corinthians 10:19–21:

What am I saying then? That an idol is anything, or what is offered to idols is anything? Rather, that the things which the Gentiles sacrifice they sacrifice to demons and not to God, and I do not want you to have fellowship with demons. You cannot drink the cup of the Lord and the cup of demons; you cannot partake of the Lord's table and of the table of demons.

If we engage in the religious rites and prayers of false and idolatrous belief systems, we are in effect opening the door to the spirits of these religions. We must renounce all false beliefs and religious acts that we have engaged in and ask the Lord to deliver us from any adverse consequences.

2. Ungodly sexual relationships

In Chapter Six we considered the issue of soul ties. These are close heart relationships which God originally intended to be a mutual blessing to all concerned. However, because of sin, these heart ties now have the potential of forging a negative bond through which the demonic can operate. Potentially a harmful soul tie might form from any ungodly or negative relationship, but the sexual tie is one of the strongest. Various forms of sexual immorality or abuse can forge very strong spiritual attachments that are used against us by the enemy.

It is imperative that we confess all ungodly relationships and associations and repent of our involvement – not only because there is obvious sin, but also because the enemy can use these soul ties as a 'channel' through which he can oppress us. Even when a relationship or an association is severed, it may well be necessary to break the potential soul tie in prayer. It is possible that soul ties predating your conversion may still be spiritually established in some way and you need to be released from such invisible bondage.

3. Unforgiveness

In Chapter Ten we looked in depth at 'The Foundation of Forgiveness'; how forgiveness is often the key to healing and deliverance. Let us remind ourselves how the enemy can use resentment and bitterness to gain a demonic foothold in our lives.

Jesus' teaching in Matthew 18:23–35 on the Unforgiving Servant warns us of the possibility of demonic 'tormenters' who will torture us if they find the legal right to do so through unforgiveness in our hearts. Also, Paul warns us in 2 Corinthians 2:10–11 that when we accommodate unforgiveness in our hearts, Satan can 'take advantage of us'. The phrase 'take advantage' has been variously translated, as we saw earlier, all translations giving us the strong impression that one of the most powerful schemes of the enemy is to overtake us in ignorance through unforgiveness. As we said before, one of the most common 'rights' that demons exploit is unforgiveness in our hearts, and the damage unforgiveness does cannot be underestimated. Unforgiveness will imprison and torture us.

If we harbour any bitterness or resentment in our hearts, it is imperative for our healing and deliverance that – as an act of our will – we forgive our offenders and release them to the justice of God. Often, it is only when we release another into the freedom of our forgiveness that we are released into freedom from the demonic bondage of spirits of judgement and unforgiveness.

4. Addictions

The normal addictive drive, whatever the particular addiction is, cannot be underestimated in its potency. We have already mentioned the addictive cycle and the adage that 'pain seeks out pleasure'. The addictive cycle is a model widely accepted, but what many are not cognisant of is the demonic element in addiction.

Of course, there are often behavioural, chemical, biological, sexual, psychological, emotional and other factors associated with an addictive pattern – but rarely is the supernatural contributor of the demonic accounted for. Addictive habits such as alcoholism, drug abuse, pornography, gambling etc. are highly addictive by their very nature, but how much more enslaving they become because of the entrance of empowering demonic forces associated with these practices!

Whenever we initially engage in sinful cycles of behaviour, and especially when this is to medicate or deaden pain, we give an almost irresistible invitation to the demonic to enter and empower our habit.

In order for some to gain complete freedom over addiction, it is often necessary not only for there to be repentance and healing but also deliverance from spirits of addiction.

5. The occult

The definition of the occult is a 'hidden' or 'secret' 'knowledge'.[1] This hidden knowledge is only for the initiated. From a biblical perspective, the occult is a forbidden knowledge. It was with forbidden knowledge that Satan tempted Adam and Eve. Deuteronomy 29:29 warns us:

> The secret things belong to the LORD our God, but those things which are revealed belong to us and to our children forever, that we may do all the words of this law.

Occult practices are condemned by God as an abomination: something God detests. There are very clear prohibitions against the occult in Deuteronomy 18:9–12:

When you come into the land which the LORD your God is giving you, you shall not learn to follow the abominations of those nations. There shall not be found among you anyone who makes his son or his daughter pass through the fire, or one who practices witchcraft, or a soothsayer, or one who interprets omens, or a sorcerer, or one who conjures spells, or a medium, or a spiritist, or one who calls up the dead. For all who do these things are an abomination to the LORD, and because of these abominations the LORD your God drives them out from before you.

At the moment, I will not elaborate on the specific details of what each of these practices entail; a quick glance at the dictionary definitions of these terms should suffice.

Certainly, in our age, there has been a popular resurgence of occult practices. I was personally aghast in the run-up to Christmas 2014 to see the 'Top Trending Toys on Google',[2] based on Google searches for toys which started trending in early October. The first four popular toys on the list were conventional items which you would expect to feature, such as dolls and Lego; however, number five on the list was the Ouija Board! Around this same time a horror film entitled *Ouija* had been released, which had obviously popularised this occult practice. What was most shocking to me was how children were being targeted in this marketing drive. In fact, when I did a quick search online, I discovered that there was much *Ouija* film memorabilia, including – wait for it – baby clothes!

There is no doubt in my mind that our society is much more ready to dabble in darkness than previous generations. I heard a Roman Catholic exorcist quoted on Sky News as saying that he didn't think the devil had upped his game, just that more were willing to play it. I'm not sure he's right, I think the devil is continually upping his game, especially as he knows his time is running out. However, I do agree that more than ever in living memory, there are people willing to play the devil's game.

If you have been dabbling in dark arts, you need to know that it is very possible you have incurred some curse that needs to be broken. Proverbs 26:2 says:

Like a flitting sparrow, like a flying swallow,
So a curse without cause shall not alight.

There are serious consequences when we open doorways of danger into the hidden realm of the occult, not least curses incurred. If you have explored this realm or have been to fortune tellers, mediums, hypnotists and the like, it is imperative that you repent of and renounce that particular activity in order to be free in Christ.

Unknowing participation in sin

Through ignorance or being forced by others, many people are snared into demonic traps. I cannot be certain, but I suspect more people are caught by the enemy's stealth than his obvious propositioning. Most people, if they knew what they were getting into, would never dance with the devil. Again, this is not an exhaustive list by any means, but it may serve to be used by the Holy Spirit to pinpoint an area of vulnerability to the demonic in your own experience.

1. Martial arts

Exercise is a worthy pastime, and there is nothing wrong with engaging in forms of self-defence either, so what could possibly be wrong with martial arts? With any activity, it is vital that we understand its origins and the philosophy of belief behind its practice.

David Cross and John Berry define martial arts as:

> Mostly associated with practices from Asia, these are combative techniques intended to bring the body into a heightened place of physical and spiritual control.[3]

The original objective of martial arts was to open oneself up to the spiritual force of strength in the universe known as the *chi*.

Often, martial arts are recommended as a form of anger management, which is ironic whenever one considers that a person will potentially open themselves up to the channelling of an even stronger anger.

Also noteworthy is the use of the Chinese or Japanese character *'do'* in many of the names for various martial arts practices, e.g. judo, aikido, tae-kwon-do. *'Do'* means 'way' or 'spiritual path'. This character is also used in the name for the ancient Chinese religion or philosophy of Taoism (or Daoism). So martial arts were never intended to be used only for physical exercise, but also for the enhancement of the whole body, soul and spirit under the authority of a spiritual 'way' other than Jesus (see John 14:6).

Do you need to repent of having unwittingly opened yourself up to alien spiritual forces through martial arts?[4]

2. Alternative therapy

When we speak of alternative therapies or medicine, we do not mean all forms of natural remedies or solutions for our health that are perhaps unconventional in terms of modern medicine. What we are referring to are methods of healing that have a particular philosophy behind them derived from the New Age or some form of Eastern Mysticism. Such alternative therapies or medicine will usually have a holistic approach to treatment, addressing the needs of body, soul and spirit. Therefore, these alternative methods of healing and wholeness are inherently spiritual. Just as in the case of marital arts, it is imperative that we ascertain what the origins of a practice are and what the belief system behind it is. Practices such as acupuncture, chakra healing, crystal therapy, hypnotherapy, certain forms of herbal medicine, massages and various meditation techniques etc. have brought many people into spiritual bondage.[5]

If we have engaged in spiritual therapies or methods of healing derived from an alternative power other than the Lord Jesus Christ, we must repent and ask the Lord to release us from any adverse consequences.

3. Yoga and Reiki

Yoga was intended to bring a person into a spiritual connection with the supreme deity of Hinduism. Yoga literally means 'yoke', and this unity with the supreme deity is achieved by meditation, breathing exercises and physical posture. It is interesting to note that many Hindu gods are animalistic in nature and many yoga exercises take on such forms.

Reiki is a form of spiritual healing in which a practitioner lays hands on the patient in order to channel healing energy to them. This form of spiritual healing has resulted in the transference of many demonic spirits.

Many people, even Christians, engage in practices such as martial arts, yoga, Reiki, acupuncture, and other alternative therapies, maintaining that they can utilise the physical and emotional benefits whilst divorcing themselves from any of the original spiritual beliefs and influences. In such cases, I often ask the question: 'Do you think the enemy got the memo on that assertion?' In other words, you may reject the spiritual side of a practice, but does the enemy recognise this and comply to your wishes? Even if you don't embrace such harmful spiritual beliefs, and yet still engage in practices that were originally spiritual in nature, do you not think it possible, nevertheless, that the enemy could gain an entrance into your life by such means?

4. Secret societies

The secrecy and unholy vows taken in many secret societies tend to bring spiritual bondage, not only to the individuals in the organisations, but to their families and even the communities in which they are prevalent.

In particular, Freemasonry is highly deceptive in how it portrays itself as an essentially charitable fraternal society, compatible with Christianity, when in fact it is a false spirituality worshipping the god 'Jah-Bul-On' (a combination of the name 'Yahweh' with the pagan deities Baal and Osiris). The diabolic genius of Freemasonry is that the truth behind this society is only revealed as you ascend the degrees. It is only at the highest level that the revelation is given that Freemasonry is, in fact, Lucifer worship. In essence, Freemasonry is classic paganism which excludes the Son of God, the only way to God: the Lord Jesus Christ.

Many other secret societies have been modelled on Freemasonry, often by Freemasons in their ranks.

We, as Christians, are to be 'children of light' (Ephesians 5:8) and are told to have no fellowship with the 'unfruitful works of darkness' (Ephesians 5:11). By their very nature, secret societies for the initiated are not Christian. Jesus said of Himself in John 18:20:

I spoke openly to the world. I always taught in synagogues and in the temple, where the Jews always meet, and in secret I have said nothing.

He told His disciples in Matthew 10:27:

Whatever I tell you in the dark, speak in the light; and what you hear in the ear, preach on the housetops.

To enjoy freedom in Christ, it is important to renounce all false beliefs, allegiances, oaths and covenants that you have entered. Some, after they are converted to Jesus, think that coming to Christ is sufficient to break the spiritual bondage of secret societies, but sometimes the oaths they have taken are only invoked in curse whenever they leave the group or divulge its secrets.

Why take a risk, when potentially so much is at stake? Repent of all involvement in any secret society and renounce it along with its false beliefs, rituals and oaths.

Breaking free

If God has spoken to you about any of these potential avenues of demonic access, why not use the prayer below to break free of the bondage and command the afflicting spirits to leave your life in Jesus' name? The Lord Jesus has given us such authority as believers. Jesus said in Luke 10:19:

Behold, I give you the authority to trample on serpents and scorpions, and over all the power of the enemy, and nothing shall by any means hurt you.

He also said in Mark 16:17:

In My name they will cast out demons ...

We have authority in Christ and power through the blood of Jesus to expel demonic influences from our lives, however they have entered. Having said that, whilst self-deliverance is possible, it may well be preferable that you acquire some assistance from trusted and competent ministers in the area of deliverance to guide you through this process.

There are some further gateways of entrance that the demonic uses to access our lives. We will consider some of these in the next couple of chapters.

A Prayer

Father, I acknowledge and confess Jesus Christ as Lord over all. I declare that at the Name of Jesus, every knee should bow, of those in heaven, and of those on earth, and of those under the earth, and that every tongue should confess that Jesus Christ is Lord, to Your glory, Father.

I surrender myself to You, spirit, soul and body. I surrender every area of my life to the Lordship of Jesus Christ alone. I renounce my pride and self-righteousness, along with any virtue that has not You as its source. I understand that I have no entitlement to Your mercy, only that Your Son died in my place.

I renounce Satan and all his works. I sever all contact I have ever had with the occult, with any secret society, or with false religion – particularly (*be specific*).

I confess the ways in which I have knowingly or ignorantly co-operated with Satan and given him a gateway into my life. Particularly, I confess (*be specific*) and I repent of these. In the Name of Jesus I ask You, Father, to please break the ungodly tie between (*insert the name of the person, place, practitioner, organisation, object etc. bringing the ungodly influence*) and I. Separate me spirit, soul and body from the effects of this ungodly tie.

Father, I thank You that on the cross Your Son Jesus was made a curse, so that I could be redeemed from every curse and instead inherit God's blessing. Because this is true, I ask that You will release me to receive the deliverance I need. I choose to identify with You, Lord Jesus, and stand against all Satan's demons. I submit my all to You, Lord, resisting the devil. Amen.

Now I speak to any demons that have had influence over me *(speak to them directly and name them if you know what they are)*[6]. I command you to go from me now, in the Name of Jesus, I expel you![7]

———•———

1. *The Oxford English Reference Dictionary, Second Edition* (Oxford: Oxford University Press, 1996).

2. Google Trends, November 2014.

3. David Cross & John Berry, *The Dangers of Alternative Ways to Healing: How to Avoid New Age Deceptions* (Lancaster: Sovereign World, 2010).

4. For more information, see Dr Vito Rallo (five-time USA National Karate Champion), *Exposing the Dangers Behind Martial Arts & Yoga* (Lancaster: Sovereign World, 2009, 2011).

5. For more information, see David Cross & John Berry, *The Dangers of Alternative Ways to Healing: How to Avoid New Age Deceptions.*

6. Often the demon's name will simply correspond to the particular behaviour it entered through or perpetuates e.g. lust, pride, greed, murder, hatred, unforgiveness, fear, control, rejection etc.

7. You may have some kind of perceptible reaction to this deliverance prayer. Some people have none and yet deliverance has taken place. Others have evident demonstrations of demonic presence or expulsion and this can vary in nature. This is when it can be helpful to have with you those who have experience in this kind of ministry. If you are on your own, try to persevere in prayer and command the spirit to leave in the Name and authority of the Lord Jesus Christ. Invoke the power of the blood of Jesus against the enemy.

CHAPTER FIFTEEN
THE UNPROFITABLE INHERITANCE

———•———

A common avenue of access into our lives which the demonic uses is what has come to be known as generational iniquity or generational curse. Basically, this is the idea that the sins of past generations can have adverse effects upon those in the present. The Hebrew word for 'iniquity' carries with it a sense of moral perverseness; the opposite of straightness (righteousness), a kind of bent and predisposition towards certain behaviours. It is believed that this can be passed down through families because of certain sins that our ancestors have engaged in. This concept is a cause of controversy for some in the Body of Christ – and no doubt, like any doctrine, it has been taken to extremes and abused. However, there is sufficient biblical data related to this subject to warrant our serious attention.

God's revelation of Himself
In history, God has been revealing Himself progressively to

humanity. This is evidenced in the lives of the biblical patriarchs and prophets. When God gave the Law to Moses, in the giving of the second commandment prohibiting the worship of idols, He declared in Exodus 20:5-6:

> ... you shall not bow down to them nor serve them. For I, the LORD your God, am a jealous God, visiting the iniquity of the fathers upon the children to the third and fourth generations of those who hate Me, but showing mercy to thousands, to those who love Me and keep My commandments.

It is notable that idolatry and false religious practices invoke this visitation on the family line (which is often still the case today). Later on, when God reissued the tablets of stone to Moses, He revealed His character through His name again as:

> The LORD, the LORD God, merciful and gracious, longsuffering, and abounding in goodness and truth, keeping mercy for thousands, forgiving iniquity and transgression and sin, by no means clearing the guilty, visiting the iniquity of the fathers upon the children and the children's children to the third and the fourth generation.
>
> *Exodus 34:6-7*

One of the greatest arguments against the idea of generational iniquity is that it is an Old Covenant concept. However, the original context of this revelation is in revealing the character of God through His name. Is God still 'merciful', 'gracious', 'longsuffering', 'abounding in goodness and truth', 'keeping mercy for thousands', 'forgiving iniquity and transgression and sin' and 'by no means clearing the guilty'? The answer is 'Yes!' He is the LORD who does not change (Malachi 3:6). Would it be sound interpretation of the Bible to extract this one trait of God – 'visiting the iniquity of the fathers upon the children and the children's children to the third and the fourth generation' – and conclude that it does not apply today? I think not. It is interesting how quickly we embrace the 'appealing' aspects of God's nature, yet how easily we reject what is uncomfortable to us!

Generational inheritance was intended by God to be a channel of repeated increased blessing. God's heart's desire is to multiply blessing upon our heads. Curse is visited on up to the third and fourth generation, but 'mercy to the thousands' (Exodus 20:6). Deuteronomy 7:9 says that God blesses to the 1000th generation of those who love Him and obey His commandments! Wow! This really reveals to us that God's heart's desire is to bless and prosper us!

Primitive dysfunctional families

Generational iniquity cannot be reserved to the Mosaic Law (the Old Covenant), as it can be observed in families before the giving of the Law. In Genesis, the book of origins, we see adverse behavioural patterns in the families of Abraham, Isaac and Jacob. There is at least a cycle of generational deceit, lying, manipulation and favouritism repeated in each era. Read the book of Genesis again and observe these and other echoing patterns of behaviour from generation to generation. Of course, the oft-asked question is: is such generational behaviour *nature* or *nurture*? Is it learned behaviour, or inherited? I think the answer is: it's probably both.

There is no doubt that we can learn certain behaviours from the examples set before us, but there is also no doubt that an element of heredity exists. We do not dispute the existence of heredity in relation to certain physical features, personality traits, natural abilities, intelligence levels and even diseases, and yet so often we exclude the possibility of there being any spiritual heredity in our family lineage.

The prophets and the sins of the fathers

In Jeremiah's day, the people of Judah rehearsed a prayer recited by Jeremiah in Lamentations 5:7:

Our fathers sinned and are no more,
But we bear their iniquities.

This is an apt description of generational iniquity. It is likely that the people were reflecting on Exodus 20:5, concluding that they were suffering for the sins of former generations. Yet we see in Israel's history a tendency to blame the sins of past generations for suffering, rather than taking ownership of their personal complicity in such sins in the present. This seems to be behind the saying recorded in Jeremiah 31:29–30:

'The fathers have eaten sour grapes
And the children's teeth are set on edge.'
But every one shall die for his own iniquity; every man who
eats the sour grapes, his teeth shall be set on edge.

Jeremiah is pointing out that generational iniquity cannot be used to exonerate us from personal guilt. We are responsible for how we have partaken of the sins of our forebears. Even Jesus referred to this when rebuking the Scribes and Pharisees:

Fill up, then, the measure of your fathers' guilt.

Matthew 23:32

Before the prayer in Lamentations ends, the people do confess their personal guilt:

> Woe to us, for we have sinned!
>
> *Lamentations 5:16*

Certainly their ancestors had helped to lead their descendants into sin, but as Warren Wiersbe puts it:

> God visits His wrath on the fathers and their children *when the children behave like their fathers!*[1]

Jeremiah 31:29–30 has been used to argue against the concept of generational iniquity. However, it does not contradict a clearly biblical principle, but rather tempers it with a sense of balance and enhances it with personal obligation. Ezekiel 18 is also used to object to this teaching:

> What do you mean when you use this proverb concerning the land of Israel, saying:
> 'The fathers have eaten sour grapes,
> And the children's teeth are set on edge'? ... The soul who sins shall die. The son shall not bear the guilt of the father, nor the father bear the guilt of the son. The righteousness of the righteous shall be upon himself, and the wickedness of the wicked shall be upon himself.
>
> *Ezekiel 18:2, 20*

Again, the context here is that God's people, with their religious knowledge of Exodus 20:5, were accusing God of being unfair and punishing them for the sins of their fathers. Their attitude was: 'No matter what we do, we still have to suffer because of what the older generation did!' God is pointing out to His people that He holds individuals guilty for their own sins and no one else's. The implication is that they were suffering for their own sins and could not blame past generations. This does not contradict Exodus 20:5. Ezekiel simply exposed how God's people were being blinded to their own personal guilt by using the sins of their fathers as an excuse. They lived with a kind of irresponsible fatalistic attitude that they couldn't change their circumstances because of what was predetermined for them by the deeds of their ancestors. Ezekiel's message was that judgement was not a fait accompli because repentance can break the ungodly cycle of generations.

However, some objectors may point out that Ezekiel explicitly stated that a son shall not bear the guilt of his father, nor the father bear the guilt of his son (Ezekiel 18:20). Surely this contradicts the idea of generational iniquity? Well, if we believe *all* Scripture to be inspired of God, we cannot favour Ezekiel 18:20 over Exodus 20:5. We must assert that God is not in the business of contradicting Himself. So what is the explanation for this apparent problem?

I believe an answer is found in viewing generational iniquity as the passing down of the *consequences* of past sins, rather than the transferring of personal *guilt* to the innocent. It is not that God holds us personally guilty for what other people did who lived long before us, but rather that there are compromising circumstances, as a result of their deeds, that we experience in our lives. The original sin of Adam and Eve is a case in point: we are not personally guilty for what Adam and Even did, yet we are all affected by the consequences of their actions.

The Old Testament prophets were also noteworthy in

confessing the sins of bygone generations because their present generation was reaping the consequences of these past sins. Nehemiah prayed:

> [I] confess the sins of the children of Israel which we have sinned against You. Both my father's house and I have sinned.
>
> *Nehemiah 1:6*

Ezra prayed:

> Since the days of our fathers to this day we have been very guilty, and for our iniquities we, our kings, and our priests have been delivered into the hand of the kings of the lands, to the sword, to captivity, to plunder, and to humiliation, as it is this day.
>
> *Ezra 9:7*

Even the psalmist prayed in Psalm 106:6:

> We have sinned with our fathers,
> We have committed iniquity ...

Generational consequences of national sin

Romans 1 teaches us that God's wrath is displayed against all ungodliness and those who 'suppress the truth in unrighteousness' (Romans 1:18). Paul goes on to teach that whenever a society does not utilise the original knowledge of God that all people had equally from the beginning, they will incur the detrimental consequences. God gives up such a society to what it wants, but that has tragic ramifications – not only for the present civilisation, but for the succeeding generations. Generations to come lose out because of the choices of previous generations. This is the explanation for many nations ending up in total spiritual darkness. As Romans 1:28 succinctly puts it:

> And even as they did not like to retain God in their knowledge, God gave them over to a debased mind, to do those things which are not fitting ...

The Western nations of the world, most of which had a Judeo-Christian spiritual and moral foundation, have rejected that heritage and are suffering the consequences we see before our very eyes. By debunking God and His Word, our post-Christian culture is now openly inviting dark principalities and powers to take a fuller role in our affairs. If this persists without God's gracious intervention, things can only get darker. This is the consequence of generational iniquity on a national scale.

To the third and fourth generation

Some take 'to the third and fourth generation' literally. If that is the case, just think how many people in that bracket might have affected us. Counting back four generations gives us four levels of ancestors: Parents – two; Grandparents – four; Great-grandparents – eight; Great-great-grandparents – sixteen; total – thirty. Any of these people could be the source of a demonic influence upon our lives. Some believe it follows that if we or another in the family line engage in the generational sin, the whole cycle will begin again.

Others take 'to the third and fourth generation' as metaphorical, simply meaning that the effects will be upon all the succeeding generations in a perpetual manner until the curse is broken.

History repeating itself

In your family line, do you recognise certain patterns, dysfunctional tendencies, premature deaths, peculiar illness, sexual aberrations, paranormal activities or abilities, addictions or dependencies? The list of the ways generational iniquity exhibits itself is potentially endless. What are you more susceptible to because of the choices of your ancestors? Can you see history repeating itself in your life experience? Spiritual power, both good and evil, can travel from one generation to another. Do you have a profitable inheritance through your family, or an unprofitable one?

Redemption in Christ[2]

Jesus Christ can break the power of your unprofitable inheritance and bring you into the blessings of being an heir of God and a joint heir with Him. This has already happened for the Christian – at least on paper – but it must be applied by faith to those areas that are still presenting generational iniquity or curse. We must appropriate the power of the blood of Jesus to gain the victory for us, our children and our children's children. There is power in the blood of Jesus to redeem us from all the consequences of our sin and inheritance.

> For you know that it was not with perishable things such as silver or gold that you were redeemed from the empty way of life handed down to you from your ancestors, but with the precious blood of Christ ...
>
> *1 Peter 1:18 (NIV UK 2011)*

When Peter refers to 'the empty way of life handed down to [them] from [their] ancestors', he is almost certainly speaking of the religious adherence to the Law of Moses. However, all of us have had 'empty' ancestral inheritances, religious, traditional, or otherwise, that have deeply affected us. Isn't it marvellous to know that whatever our unprofitable inheritance has been, the blood of Jesus can redeem us and set us free?

A Prayer

Father, I come to You as the Father after whom all the families in heaven and earth are named. You originally ordained the family to be a blessing on the succeeding generations and I thank You for the blessings in my life derived from the righteousness of bygone generations.

Though Your intention through the family was blessing, through some of the sins of my ancestors, iniquity and curse may have been visited upon me and my family. In the Name of the Lord Jesus Christ I choose to forgive my forebears for their sins that have harmed me. I confess any way that I have engaged in those same sins. I renounce those sins *(specify if you know them)* and I ask You to cut me off from any iniquity and curse coming down to me through either my mother's or my father's family line.

I thank You, Father, that the Lord Jesus Christ took all my curse on the cross. I ask You to set me free from every curse upon my life and family, that I might inherit God's blessing. In the Name of the Lord Jesus Christ and by the power of His blood, I command any demonic spirits carrying generational iniquity or curse to me and my family to leave me now! Amen.

———•———

1. Warren W. Wiersbe, *The Bible Exposition Commentary: Old Testament: The Prophets* (Colorado Springs, CO: Victor, 2002).

2. 'Redemption' or 'to redeem' simply means 'to buy something back'. In Bible times, the term was used when referring to buying back from slavery.

CHAPTER SIXTEEN
THE FEAR FACTOR

———•———

One of the primary ways the enemy gains admittance into our lives is through fear. We have already explored some of the ways that wounds can affect us. Wounds, as well as sins, can open up avenues for the demonic to gain a foothold in our lives. Whenever a person experiences a particularly traumatic event (such as an accident, for example), their deep pain and vulnerability in that moment can create an opportunity for an evil spirit to enter, reinforcing their pattern of brokenness. In addition to accidents, there are many other scenarios in which a person can be susceptible to attacks from spirits of fear or trauma, perhaps through bereavement, or physical or sexual abuse.

Trauma and fear issues can be particularly pronounced in communities that have experienced excessive violence or war. My own country of Northern Ireland is a case in point, having experienced many years of 'The Troubles'. Many involved in the conflict, whatever their role may have been, were at times exposed to some very shocking scenes. Even children who grew up through those years were accustomed to a certain 'normality' which, with hindsight, was not normal at all.

It is only in later years that the long-term effects of such national conflicts become evident. Similar ramifications can be observed in other communities which have witnessed much trauma, perhaps through natural disasters, industrial tragedies (such as mining or fishing accidents), slavery, or even the prevalence of witchcraft in the culture. I am convinced that in such circumstances, healing and deliverance may be needed for whole families, the Church, and even the wider community, in order to receive release on many levels from the oppression the enemy has caused.[1]

Epidemic fear

According to phobialist.com,[2] there are around 530 phobias in existence, with an estimated 10 million people in the UK claiming to suffer from one. That's incredible, when you consider that the population of the UK is around 65 million. Fear is a particular problem in the lives of many Christians. It often appears to remain unchallenged, because we don't consider it as serious a sin as other immoral practices; it appears more sanitised! Yet God's Word is clear, 2 Timothy 1:7:

> For God has not given us a spirit of fear, but of power and of love and of a sound mind.

So, if God hasn't given us a spirit of fear, where does it come from? If someone other than God is giving us this spirit, why would we want it?

Good fear vs. bad fear

There are certain fears that are good. Scripture has much to say about the need to 'fear God' (around 300 verses). The fear of the Lord warrants a whole study on its own, but essentially it is a loving and submissive awe and reverence towards God. It is not to be confused with a terrifying fear, where we are negatively intimidated by God. Naturally, if God showed up in all His glory and power, I don't think any of us could survive it, let alone stay composed and unafraid. However, when we are in Christ, we are in a love relationship with the Father through Jesus, and, when abiding in Him, 1 John 4:18 becomes a reality:

> There is no fear in love. But perfect love drives out fear, because fear has to do with punishment. The one who fears is not made perfect in love.
>
> *(NIV UK 2011)*

A wrong fear of God comes from being under the Law and fearing His punishment because you see yourself as a transgressor. Jesus, through His death on the cross, has exhausted the wrath of God towards our sins – therefore, if Jesus is our Saviour, there is no punishment to fear. The true fear of the Lord, then, is a loving dependence upon God's love in our lives and a devoted reverence towards God our Father.

Another good fear, to a degree, is natural fear. Fear, per se, is not inherently bad. It has been given to us by God as a kind of safety mechanism to protect us. God has created us with a biological nervous system which gathers, stores and responds to stimuli. We react to danger with 'the fight or flight response': a physiological reaction that occurs in response to a perceived harmful event, attack, or threat to survival. Even before we cross a road, we look right and left to check that there are no cars coming in our direction. When placing a log on a fire, we are careful not to get our hand burned. God has given us natural fear as a gift to protect us, but like many of God's blessings it has often been perverted and empowered by the enemy. Fear is a very powerful emotion (like sexual attraction) and so the enemy knows he can easily use it to his benefit and our destruction.

The real problem comes when fear ceases to be our servant and becomes our master, as we heed unnatural and disproportionate fears. To continue with the example above: if we *won't even cross the road* lest we get run over by a car – there's a serious problem. Eventually we won't even venture out of the house, lest something fatal takes place. Again, if we *won't even light the fire* for fear that we will burn down the house, fear has now become a stronghold in our lives. What God has given to us as a gift to protect us and those we love can become not only a chemical addiction to us, but a demonic empowerment.

We have observed how traumatic events can open the doorway to spirits of fear, but so can persistently giving way to unnatural and disproportionate fears. Fear consequently becomes supernatural in its enslaving control of us. A 'spirit of fear', then, is not only the human spirit in a fearful disposition, but can be an actual demonic entity whose assignment against us is to engender and establish fear in our hearts.

The mechanics of fear

Many are ignorant of how fear works. Fear is essentially a kind of 'separation anxiety' resulting from being separated from God. The first mention of fear in the Bible is in Genesis 3. Adam and Eve had sinned and God was looking for them. Genesis records that they hid themselves from God's presence and Adam responded to God by saying:

I heard Your voice in the garden, and I was afraid because I was naked; and I hid myself.

Genesis 3:10

Sin brought separation between Adam and Eve, and God. There was a loss of protection and security, into which primal fear entered. Here is an important principle to understand: when humanity lost its relationship with God, the spiritual covering of protection was also lost. Fear entered the human heart when, through sin, the covering of protection was forfeited. The original sin happened when Adam and Eve believed the devil's lie, and fear enters our lives when we believe the lies Satan tells us. When we believe Satan's lies we, as it were, enter into a contract with him, giving him certain powers over us. Any time you believe the lie, you empower the liar. At the root of every controlling fear there is a lie. That lie will move from the mind, where it has first been embraced ('I think this is true'), to the emotions, where it is then felt ('this feels true'), to the will, where it will be acted upon in a way that negatively transforms behaviours. If the fear is embraced as one's actual identity, it can distort the human spirit – then the lie effectively becomes a part of you. This may well be what takes place with some who have debilitating phobias.

So, to summarise a little: through believing the devil's lies, we become spiritually uncovered and can give place to spirits of fear, bringing us into deep spiritual bondage. It may have been through an accident or traumatic event that we believed the lie that God wasn't in control or protecting us as He should have been, and then a spirit of fear entered us. Psalm 91 is a wonderful prayer which helps us overcome fear. It begins with the words:

He who dwells in the secret place of the Most High
Shall abide under the shadow of the Almighty.

Psalm 91:1

In other words, the ultimate place of safety is to abide under the protective canopy of God's shadow. We need to choose to trust God's protective covering. Under His wing we are safe, but when we choose to step out from under His wing through believing the lies of Satan, then we become exposed to demonic attack.

The spiritual principle of covering is an important one. God ultimately is the covering of every one of His children, and we can dwell in safety under His wing, regardless of what our earthly relationships have been like. However, there are certain established protocols God has set in order. For instance, Christ covers His Church, but He has chosen to administer that covering in some ways through human leadership. When the leadership covering is compromised somehow (perhaps through sin, pride or apostasy), it can expose the flock of God to attacks from the enemy. Also, husbands are meant to operate in a kind of covering over their wives and, likewise, parents over their children. So, whenever husbands, fathers and mothers are not what they should be, families can be spiritually harmed.

Exposed?

If you struggle with abnormal levels of fear, you should ask the question: 'When and where did my life get out from under covering?' When were you spiritually exposed? How did you become vulnerable and wide open to the attack of spirits of fear?

Maybe there isn't a living memory you have of any event, but there was some trauma in your family or ancestral lineage which has been passed down to you. Perhaps your mother was particularly fearful during a difficult pregnancy, or you had a very traumatic birth into the world which has affected you. Or it could be that in your own experience, you can readily identify a life trauma, accident, abusive incident, or a brush with disaster or darkness that established this stronghold of fear.

Get covered

In order to be ultimately set free from paralysing fear, you will need to receive God's covering over your life. You must relinquish all ungodly control you have exerted over yourself to keep yourself safe, and you will need to decide – by an act of your will – to trust God alone to protect you. Of course, this will be counter to your emotions, which have become conditioned by fear. They will vociferously object to surrendering to God, telling you that you will be exposed to danger again. You must ignore these further lies and choose, by a raw act of your will, to believe God.

Ultimately, it will be in knowing who you are in Christ (your true identity) and who God is as your *Abba* Father that will give you the sense of security and safety to trust Him. Ask the Holy Spirit now to reveal to you what is in the heart of God the Father towards you. Romans 8:15 describes this well:

> For you did not receive the spirit of bondage again to fear,
> but you received the Spirit of adoption by whom we cry out,
> 'Abba, Father.'

It is in knowing that we are not vulnerable orphans but sons and daughters of our Father God that we will be brought into a safe place of covering and trust. Then 'power, love and a sound mind' will be ours, rather than bondage to the fear spirit.

Expose the lie

Another thing necessary in overcoming the spirit of fear is to identify the lie you believed in that moment when you felt your covering of protection was compromised. You will need to renounce that lie to be set free. Jesus said in John 8:32:

> Then you will know the truth, and the truth will set you free.
> *(NIV UK 2011)*

We must identify and confess lies underlying our fears – the lies that have created the strongholds of the mind in which the enemy hides. We must renounce these and replace them with the truth of what God says.

What about worry?

Showing concern about things we value is normal. Indeed, concern is a good motivator to be careful about people and things we value. It is natural to be nervous about sitting an exam, or visiting the doctor or dentist. However, when concern for something future (with an unknown outcome) prevents us functioning today, something is seriously wrong.

Worry robs us today by stressing about tomorrow. This is why Jesus, in the Sermon on the Mount, commands three times, 'do not worry' (Matthew 6:25, 31, 34). He concludes His point on worry by exhorting:

> Therefore do not worry about tomorrow, for tomorrow will worry about itself. Each day has enough trouble of its own.
> *Matthew 6:34 (NIV UK 2011)*

Corrie ten Boom, in the last few years of her life, said:

Worry does not empty tomorrow of sorrows; it empties today of its strength.[3]

Worry should be disposed of, because it doesn't work! It is based on assumptions, rather than facts. Someone developed the excellent acrostic for fear: False, Evidence, Appearing, Real. It has been said that just under half of the things we worry about never happen, and most of the rest of what we worry about has already happened and therefore can't be changed! Worry is an utter waste of our time and precious energies. This is why Jesus asked in Matthew 6:27:

Which of you by worrying can add one cubit to his stature?

Sin is sin!

When Jesus says, 'Don't worry', we have to take Him seriously and obey. Not to obey is sin. In order to gain victory over fear and worry, we need to view these as God sees them. We must recognise these as sin which is never excusable. This is one of the reasons we don't get victory in this area, because we are not ruthless with fear and worry as sins. Billy Sunday once said:

One reason sin flourishes is that it is treated like a cream puff instead of a rattlesnake.[4]

It is not excusable to say, 'Oh, my mother was a worrier, and granny was a worrier, and I've just got the genes.' Whilst worry and fear issues can be passed through the generations, and also learned by the examples we have been set, we must view them mercilessly and stop making excuses for them. These are not simply personality defects, these are sin. John Wesley said:

I would no more fret than to curse or swear.[5]

Let's face it: anything that robs us of the peace of God must be sin, and what has this effect upon us more than fear and worry? We must rob the enemy of the authority he has gained in our lives by any compliance with, or accommodation of, fear and worry in our lives. If there are generational dimensions to these issues, renounce them, but be ready to take ownership of your own personal participation with such spirits.

Tell fear where to go

If spirits of fear, worry, or trauma have gained entrance into your life, it is imperative that – having followed the steps already outlined in this chapter – you then command those spirits to leave you. Forgiveness towards those who may have caused or taught you fear might also need to take place (see Chapter Ten).

Choose to walk in faith, not fear

We must obey the most frequent command in the Bible: 'Fear not!' Some say it's in the Bible 365 times, one for every day of the year! Fear and faith are similar: both are the belief that something that hasn't happened is going to happen. Fear is the belief that something bad is going to happen, faith is the belief that what God has said will happen. Hebrews 11:1 defines faith as:

   ... the substance of things hoped for, the evidence of things not seen.

Faith is focusing on God's truth; fear and worry is meditating on the enemy's lies. Imagine what our faith levels would be like if we used all the mental and emotional energy that we normally expend on anxiety and invested it in meditating on truth! Paul tells us to do this in Philippians 4:6, 8:

> Be anxious for nothing ... Finally, brethren, whatever things are true, whatever things are noble, whatever things are just, whatever things are pure, whatever things are lovely, whatever things are of good report, if there is any virtue and if there is anything praiseworthy – meditate on these things.

What environment do we create in our minds? What are we flooding our minds with via media, music, literature, etc.? Do we have a mental diet which is fear-inducing or faith-building? We need to turn off the taps that flood our minds with fear, and turn on the taps that will flood our minds with the water of the Word.

Have a plan of action

Whilst people can, in a moment, be delivered of a spirit of fear or anxiety, I have discovered that usually those who gain and maintain long-term freedom are the ones who have embraced life-changing renewal of the mind *and also* have a strategy to counteract the advance of fear. There needs to be a plan of action that you implement whenever attacks of fear occur.

One plan of action I've found helpful is to realise that potentially, every day of my life, I could have two different postmen come to the door of my mind: one from the devil and the other from God. My default was to automatically receive the lies of the devil – every day, without question – and begin to entertain, dissect and analyse those lies, to the destruction of my peace. I resolved that I would choose God's delivery filled with His truth, and meditate on it. At the beginning this was hard, but it was a strategy that worked. It is in the midst of fear that we must choose to believe God. We have to make a choice contrary to what our emotions are saying.

The devil is afraid of your fearlessness

I remember hearing a well-known preacher[6] commenting on Philippians 1:28:

> ... and not in any way terrified by your adversaries, which is to them a proof of perdition, but to you of salvation, and that from God.

He said something along the lines that every time we are victorious over a fear issue in our lives, what is broadcast over the PA system of hell is impending doom. The demons try to get us to fear, so they don't have to think about what's coming to them! Wow! No wonder the powers of darkness work so hard to get us to fear. What a huge incentive for us to tell the demons of fear to get out of our lives in Jesus' Name!

Someone has said well: 'Fear kills more dreams than failure ever will.'[7] Imagine, what would you do if you had no fear?

A Prayer

Father, I renounce all ungodly control over my life, submit to You, and receive Your covering of love and protection. I thank You that You are my great and good Abba Father.

Lord Jesus, in Your Name, I confess and renounce all fear, anxiety, doubt and unbelief. Forgive me for believing the lies of Satan, that (*identify the lies*). I reject these and choose to believe the truth that (*declare the truth of God's Word*).

I freely choose to forgive (*name if you can*) for how they made me afraid. I ask You, Lord, to break all ungodly soul ties with (*name if you can*). Lord, I ask You to heal my emotions, my memories and all damage that fear has done in my life.

From this moment, I choose to listen to Your voice alone and meditate on the truth of the good things in Your Word. Now, in the Name and authority of the Lord Jesus Christ, I command all demonic spirits of fear, worry, trauma, unbelief and doubt to leave me now! I speak directly to all demonic spirits who have had any influence over me and, in Jesus' Name, I expel you.

I ask You, Lord Jesus, to now fill me with Your Holy Spirit and all His good fruit – especially His love, joy, peace and faith. Thank You, Lord. Amen.

————•————

1. In the biblical record, it appears that serious sin can release spiritual consequences upon the land by strengthening ruling spirits in the heavenly realm. The four areas of sin that are said to bring bondage and pollution to the land are: *idolatry* (Jeremiah 3:1; 16:18), *bloodshed* (Numbers 35:33), *occult practices* (Deuteronomy 18:9–12) and *sexual immorality*

(Leviticus 18:1–30). There needs to be great wisdom shown by the Church whenever seeking to address such territorial strongholds. An individual Christian should not seek to 'take on' such spiritual forces on their own. Ideally, a representation of the Body of Christ in a vicinity should seek to weaken such powers – not by direct engagement, but through repentance, reconciliation and coming to people in the community (especially those traditionally considered their enemies) in the opposite spirit of love and grace etc.

2. Accessed 17.7.17.

3. www.goodreads.com/quotes/35574-worry-does-not-empty-tomorrow-of-its-sorrow-it-empties (accessed 7.8.17).

4. Billy Sunday, www.goodreads.com/quotes/190656 (accessed 17.7.17).

5. John R. Rice, *Prayer: Asking and Receiving* (Murfreesboro: Sword of the Lord, 1942).

6. Bill Johnson at Ealing Christian Centre, London, May 2015.

7. Suzy Kassem, www.goodreads.com/quotes/5019267 (accessed 17.7.17).

CHAPTER SEVENTEEN
GETTING FREE AND STAYING FREE!

———•———

Having now imbibed so much information on *sins, wounds* and *demons,* do you sense that the Holy Spirit has been diagnosing certain barriers to blessing in your life? Have blockages to your spiritual growth been identified? Perhaps you have been able to pinpoint the invisible and malevolent hindrance that somehow is wedged between you and intimacy with God, your Father. It is my prayer that through the Holy Spirit's interaction with you in this book, and especially in the prayers that you have prayed at the end of each chapter, you will already have experienced a measure of breakthrough. However, the process of healing and deliverance is often progressive, and we must, therefore, be prepared to navigate the course upon which the Holy Spirit guides us. None of us is the finished article, we are all on a continuing journey, being transformed into the likeness of God's Son. It is vital that we persevere on this journey and allow the

Lord, in His own gentle way, to probe the depths of our sin and pain, to uncover the hidden things, so that He can complete the work of healing and release which He has begun in us.

Let me repeat the warning I gave in the Introduction: it is important that you don't become introspective and begin to apply everything in this book to yourself. Some people can be very impressionable and the enemy can use this to overwhelm them with problems they don't actually have. Remember, Satan is the 'accuser of [the] brethren' (Revelation 12:10) – he will accuse us of issues we have and even ones we don't have; whichever works best for his soul-destroying purposes! So, don't allow the enemy to torment you about phantom problems. Having said that, if God has witnessed that there could be a problem in the areas of *sins*, *wounds* and *demons*, you must deal with this before the Lord in order to know the liberty and life that is God's will for you in Christ Jesus.

No 'no man's land'

There is no such a thing as 'spiritual neutrality'. In the spiritual war being waged for our souls, you are either *for* or *against* Jesus Christ. Whilst, in their minds, some 'moderate' and 'moral' people may think they do not oppose Christ, the fact of the matter is: if they are not completely *for* Christ, they are in a perilous spiritual position. Jesus said in Matthew 12:30:

> He who is not with Me is against Me, and he who does not gather with Me scatters abroad.

The context of this statement by Jesus was His teaching related to the vacating movements of demonic spirits after deliverance has taken place. He reveals in Matthew 12:43–45:

When an unclean spirit goes out of a man, he goes through dry places, seeking rest, and finds none. Then he says, 'I will return to my house from which I came.' And when he comes, he finds it empty, swept, and put in order. Then he goes and takes with him seven other spirits more wicked than himself, and they enter and dwell there; and the last state of that man is worse than the first. So shall it also be with this wicked generation.

Much revelation related to the nation of Israel at the time and to the workings of deliverance could be derived from this portion of Scripture. However, the one point I want to emphasise is: whatever else Jesus is teaching here, He is certainly warning us, 'Beware of an empty life!' Even after deliverance, if a vacuum has been created, the demonic will seek to gain a foothold once more in order to fill the life again. An empty life is a standing invitation for Satan to go to work. Banish the thought that you can remain 'blissfully', 'nominally', Christian.

Remember Ananias and Sapphira (Acts 5:1ff) who, having sold their field, gave the impression that they had given all the proceeds to the Church when, in fact, they held some back? They obviously thought they could be 95 per cent obedient to God, but remain safely disobedient in one small area without consequence. They were gravely deceived. The plot of greed in their heart was a patch big enough for Satan to gain a stronghold, and from there he filled their hearts (see Acts 5:3). There is no such thing as spiritual 'no man's land', so we must beware of an empty life.

Possessed by God

It is imperative that we receive the Spirit-immersed life Jesus died to purchase for us. This life is the promise of the Father and the Son, that they would send the Holy Spirit, 'another' of the same kind as Jesus, who would be our 'Strengthener/Encourager' (see John 14:16). As the Lord Jesus announced His departure to the disciples, He assured them He would not leave them 'orphans', but would come to them by the Holy Spirit (John 14:18). The Holy Spirit was sent at Pentecost (Acts 2) to completely possess us. Having received the gift of the Spirit when we are born again (John 3:3), God wants to inhabit us entirely as His temples (1 Corinthians 6:19). It is vital for our healing and holiness that we receive from the Father, in Jesus' Name, all of the Spirit's ministry that God has for us. Christianity is only authentic whenever lived in the fullness of the dynamic power of the Holy Spirit; it wasn't designed to work otherwise! It is vital that your life is filled with the life of God in the Holy Spirit.

Take out the trash!

In his day, King Hezekiah cleared out the rubbish from the Temple of the LORD. We read in 2 Chronicles 29:16:

> The Priests started from the inside and worked out; they emptied the place of the accumulation of defiling junk – pagan rubbish that had no business in that holy place …
>
> *(The Message)*

The Lord Jesus, when cleansing the Temple,[1] demonstrated that God wants to dwell completely present in His vessels, but often there is the 'accumulation of defiling junk – pagan rubbish that [has] no business' in the holy places of our lives now redeemed by the blood of Jesus.

Are you prepared to allow the Lord to sweep clean the

sanctuary of your life 'from the inside out', so that He may take up residence?

Following through

When Paul ministered in Ephesus, we discover that God worked great supernatural signs through the apostle, including many deliverances from evil spirits. We read in Acts 19 that some itinerant Jewish exorcists, along with the seven sons of the Jewish chief priest Sceva, took it upon themselves to mimic the method of Paul in exorcising a demonised man in the Name of Jesus. It did not go well for them! Acts 19:15–16 reads:

> And the evil spirit answered and said, 'Jesus I know, and Paul I know; but who are you?' Then the man in whom the evil spirit was leaped on them, overpowered them, and prevailed against them, so that they fled out of that house naked and wounded.

As Christians, we *do* have authority to expel demons (Luke 10:19; Mark 16:17), but these itinerants and the sons of Sceva weren't operating under the authority of Christ. It appears they adopted what they thought was simply a technique Paul had successfully used, invoking the Name of Jesus. Though we have authority in Christ over the powers of darkness, this account still serves as a warning to us all not to be careless as we engage with our formidable enemy. We should never be intimidated by the enemy, but neither should we be recklessly foolhardy when we encounter the demonic. We must ensure that we are up to date in our confession of sin to God, abiding in Christ, and adorned by the armour of God for protection. Yes, we overcome Satan by the blood of the Lamb and the word of our testimony (Revelation

12:11), but we must make certain that the enemy has no claims on us when we do battle with him.

It was this violent incident with these 'wannabe exorcists' that triggered fear among the Ephesian believers. We read in Acts 19:18–19:

> Also many of those who were now believers came, confessing and divulging their practices. And a number of those who had practised magic arts brought their books together and burned them in the sight of all. And they counted the value of them and found it came to fifty thousand pieces of silver.
> *(ESV UK)*

It appears that some of these believers, after their conversion, had retained remnants of their pagan past, some even continuing to dabble in elements of darkness. However, when they witnessed the work of the destructive demonic power behind their 'cultural indulgences', they freaked out! They brought their secret practices into the open and disposed of all the related paraphernalia. They even had what is, perhaps, one of the most expensive bonfires in history. Luke records that the value of the magic books they burned was 'fifty thousand pieces of silver', which is 50,000 drachma. One drachma was one day's wage at that time – if we take a day's wage in the UK today to be around £95, that would mean the equivalent value of what the Ephesians incinerated is somewhere around £4,750,000! That was a high price to pay for freedom, but I suppose the Ephesians had calculated that ultimately it would cost them more to stay in league with the enemy!

It is very instructive to note the knock-on effect of the Ephesians' drastic action, Acts 19:20:

So the word of the Lord grew mightily and prevailed.

Of course, this refers to a city in spiritual awakening, but it could also be applied to an individual life. The Word of God will grow mightily and prevail in our lives if we get rid of the rubbish! So, is there any trash that you need to take out of your life, out of your home, out of your marriage, or out of your church?

To get free and *stay free*, we need to be drastic with the avenues of entrance the enemy has gained in our lives.

Staying free

Healing and deliverance ministry must not be practised in isolation from the normal process of Christian discipleship. The pursuit of God as faithful followers of Jesus Christ is foundational to the successful long-term outcome of all ministry received. We have seen from Matthew 12 that spirits do desire to return to their former home in the delivered person. This cannot happen if the believer closes all the doors once opened to the enemy and walks close to the Lord, refusing the devil another foothold. Remember:

> ... He who is in you [Jesus, by the Holy Spirit] is greater than he who is in the world [Satan].
>
> *1 John 4:4*

Some people need to return again and again to receive deliverance, because the enemy regains entry. What can be done to prevent this from happening?

In conclusion, let me briefly share some further simple guidelines to help you stay free once you gain your freedom in Christ.

1. Submit to and co-operate with the Holy Spirit's renewal of your mind

Allow the Lord to change your mind and align your thoughts to what your identity is now in Christ and what He says about you. Sometimes, after deliverance, people feel a kind of identity crisis, because they sense they have lost something within them that they closely identified with. Therefore, after deliverance, it is vital that our identity is quickly rooted in who we are in Christ. We must give priority to meditating on these truths and not the lies of the enemy (Philippians 4:8). The decision to do this must be our own; no one can co-operate with the Holy Spirit for us in the renewing of our minds.

2. Be on your guard against temptations to sin

Healthy boundaries should be put in place to help prevent us falling easily into our old sinful ways. It may be helpful to have an accountability partner or structure in place to give you support in this. We should also be aware of the times we are most vulnerable to relapsing. Addiction counsellors have used the acrostic 'H.A.L.T.' to help us recognise when we are more vulnerable – when we are Hungry, Angry, Lonely or Tired. You may have personal pressure points that make you more susceptible to sin. Get to know yourself and your own weaknesses.

3. Get into a supportive community of Christians

The Body of Christ is God's original blueprint for a support group. Fellowship is indispensable for every Christian, not least those who are receiving healing and deliverance. Whilst we want to continue to influence our non-Christian friends with the gospel, it is imperative that we also cultivate Christian fellowship for mutual encouragement (see Hebrews 10:24–25).

4. Cultivate the practice of forgiving the offences of others

We spent plenty of space in Chapter Ten considering the importance of forgiveness in receiving healing and being set free. Ongoing forgiveness is necessary to maintain your freedom. This is particularly relevant in situations where offence continues to be committed against us.

5. Get immersed in and be continually filled with the Holy Spirit

Ask the Lord, by faith, to immerse you in the power of His Holy Spirit (Luke 11:13). Continue to receive the infilling of His Spirit moment by moment as you abide in Him (Ephesians 5:18).

6. Keep abiding in the love of God the Father

It is the love of the Father we are all searching for, even when we don't realise it. The 'love tanks'[2] of our hearts can only be filled and fully satisfied through Father's love. We need to saturate ourselves in the truth of 'the Father heart of God' and allow the Lord to do a deep work in us through His Spirit of adoption. Jude 21 exhorts us:

... keep yourselves in the love of God ...

Or, as *The Message* renders it:

... staying right at the center of God's love ...

It is our being centred in the love of God the Father that will cause us to continue in healing and help us mature as believers. Whatever other strategies we may use to stay free, however sophisticated they may be, if the Father's love is not at the centre, all of them will eventually fail.

7. Seek to walk in loving devotion to God's will in His Word

Legalistic obedience is not our aim, but rather a loving devotion from our hearts. As our relationship with the Father grows, the true fear of the Lord will possess us and we will only ever want to bring joy to our *Abba* Father. We must choose, in love, to do God's will according to His Word; walking in the light and agreeing with His truth (see 1 John 2:5–6).

8. Put on the armour of God and resist the devil

In Ephesians 6:10–18, Paul tells us of the supernatural provision of the armour of God which every believer in Christ can avail themselves of. We are in a battle. As soldiers of Christ, we need to utilise, by faith, each piece of God's armour as we war against the enemy. It would be highly beneficial to do a personal study of Ephesians 6, as each item has a significant practical element to it that will equip us further in our spiritual warfare.[3] Every day, we should seek to prayerfully dress ourselves in this armour as we strive to resist the enemy's advances in our lives. We must not be passive, but active in our spiritual fight. It is not in *our* strength that we take on the enemy, but in the 'power of His might' (Ephesians 6:10); nevertheless, *we* are to fight!

Victory is assured when we submit to the Lord Jesus Christ and follow His ways, as He leads us by His Spirit – then we can know complete and final triumph over the enemy in our lives. This is how we will break through every barrier and into God's blessing for us.

The apostle James summarises the whole matter succinctly by encouraging us to:

> Submit yourselves therefore to God. Resist the devil, and he *will* flee from you.
>
> *James 4:7 (KJV, emphasis mine)*

A Prayer

Father, I give You praise for my Saviour, the Lord Jesus Christ, and I thank You deeply for the great work You have begun in my life. I trust in You to bring that work to completion and perfection. I am so grateful for the healing and deliverance I have received.

Father, I choose to dispose of anything that is a hindrance to Your blessing in my life. Help me to be ruthless with any compromise I have made with the enemy.

Father, I want to *get free* and *stay free*! To that end, I agree to submit to and co-operate with the Holy Spirit's renewal of my mind, according to Your truth. I accept my identity 'in Christ' and from now on I choose to meditate on the truth of Your Word rather than the lies of the devil.

Please make me aware of my own weaknesses to temptation and sin, and give me the courage and wisdom to resist. I also pray for good Christian fellowship and a healthy church family where I will be accepted and nurtured as a child of God.

Father, please give me grace to continually forgive others for their offences towards me, so that the enemy will not gain a foothold in my life through bitterness. Give me Your supernatural love for others. I can only experience this love if I am abiding in the Father's love moment by moment. Keep me centred in Your love, *Abba* Father. Let me live a life of obedience outflowing from devotion to You. May it be Your love, Father, that always satisfies me and fills any emptiness within me.

Lord Jesus, please completely immerse me in Your Holy Spirit and continually fill my inner being with Your life and power, so that I may have the strength to live as You have called me.

By faith, I put on the whole armour of God to stand against Satan's attacks. I dress myself with *the belt of truth, the breastplate of righteousness, the shoes of the preparation of the gospel of peace, the shield of faith, the helmet of salvation, the sword of the Spirit* and *all kinds of prayer.* Cover me with the power of the precious blood of the Lamb and give Your holy angels charge to keep me in all of Your ways.

I pray this all with thanksgiving, in the Name of the Lord Jesus Christ. Amen.

---

1. Jesus probably cleansed the Temple on two occasions: at the beginning and the end of His earthly ministry (John 2; Matthew 21).

2. Gary Chapman, *The 5 Love Languages* (Chicago, IL: Northfield Publishing, 2015).

3. A good and practical assessment of the armour of God is found in Neil T. Anderson, *The Bondage Breaker* (Oxford: Monarch, 1990).

APPENDIX
LORDSHIP PRAYER[1]

———————

Lord Jesus Christ, I confess You now as my Lord, my Saviour, my Redeemer and my Deliverer. I welcome You now to be Lord of every area of my life.

Be Lord of my spirit – of my worship, my conscience, and my spiritual perception.

Be Lord of my mind – of my thoughts, my understanding, and my imagination.

Be Lord of my emotions and each feeling I experience.

Be Lord of my will – of my choices and motives, of my plans and all my intentions.

Be Lord of my body and of my health, all my actions and all my senses:

– **of my sight** and the things I would look at, along with every look that I give out

– **of my hearing** and all that I listen to

– **of my speech** and conversation, and of everything that enters my mouth.

Be Lord of my sexuality in all its expressions.

Be Lord of my hands, the tasks that they engage in, and anything they touch.

Be Lord of my feet, each step they take, and every path that I travel.

Be Lord of my finances, as they come in and go out, and of all my belongings.

Be Lord of my time – of my labour, my leisure, my sleep, and my dreams.

Be Lord of my relationships – of my friends, my co-workers, my church, (my marriage) and my family.

Be Lord of my ambitions and any plans for my future.

Be Lord of the timing of my passing from this world to the next.

Lord Jesus, I thank You for shedding Your blood, that I might be cleansed and set free. I place myself into Your hands, spirit, soul and body.

Amen.

———•———

1. This prayer is based on one used by Ellel Ministries.

FOR FURTHER
READING

Anger: How Do You Handle It?
Paul & Liz Griffin, Sovereign World, 2006.

Blessing Or Curse: You Can Choose
Derek Prince, DPM, 1990.

Demon Possession and the Christian: A New Perspective
C. Fred Dickason, Moody, 1987.

Experiencing Father's Embrace
Jack Frost, Destiny Image, 2002.

Explaining Deliverance
Graham Dow, Sovereign World, 2003.

Exposing the Dangers Behind Martial Arts & Yoga
Dr Vito Rallo, Sovereign World, 2011.

Forgiveness – God's Master Key
Peter Horrobin, Sovereign World, 2008.

Freedom From Fear
Neil T. Anderson & Rich Miller, Monarch, 1999.

God's Covering: A Place of Healing
David Cross, Sovereign World, 2008.

God's Remedy For Rejection
Derek Prince, Whitaker House, 1993.

Healing Through Deliverance
Peter Horrobin, Sovereign World, 1991.

Hope And Healing For The Abused
Paul & Liz Griffin, Sovereign World, 2007.

Illusions Of Intimacy: Unmasking Patterns of Sexual Addiction and Bringing Deep Healing to Those Who Struggle
Signa & Conlee Bodishbaugh, Sovereign World, 2004.

Intercession and Healing: Breaking Through with God
Fiona Horrobin, Sovereign World, 2008.

Letting God Be Judge: Recognizing the Impact of Ungodly Judgments and Dealing with Them
Thomas J. Sappington, Sovereign World, 2008.

Listening Prayer: Learning to Hear God's Voice and Keep a Prayer Journal
Leanne Payne, Baker, 1994.

Living Free in Christ
Dr Neil T. Anderson, Monarch, 1993.

Living in the Freedom of the Spirit
Tom Marshall, Sovereign World, 2001.

Loved Like Never Before – Discovering The Father Heart Of God
Ken Symington, Sovereign World, 2011.

Needless Casualties Of War
John Paul Jackson, Streams, 1999.

Overcoming Depression
Neil T. & Joanne Anderson, Regal, 2004.

Rescue From Rejection
Denise Cross, Sovereign World, 2010.

Restoring the Christian Soul
Leanne Payne, Baker, 1991.

Sex: God's Truth
Jill Southern, Sovereign World, 2006.

Soul Ties: The Unseen Bond in Relationships
David Cross, Sovereign World, 2006.

Sound Judgement: What Judging Is, When We Should Do It and How
Derek Prince, DPM, 2002.

Spiritual Slavery to Sonship
Jack and Trisha Frost, Destiny Image, 2016.

The Broken Image: Restoring Personal Wholeness Through Healing Prayer
Leanne Payne, Baker, 1981.

The Danger of Alternative Ways to Healing – How to Avoid New Age Deceptions
David Cross & John Berry, Sovereign World, 2010.

The Healing Presence: Curing the Soul Through Union with Christ
Leanne Payne, Baker, 1995.

The Journey to Wholeness in Christ: A Devotional Adventure To Becoming Whole
Signa Bodishbaugh, Chosen, 1997.

The Power of a New Identity
Dan Sneed, Sovereign World, 2000.

The Utter Relief of Holiness: How God's Goodness Frees us from Everything That Plagues Us
John Eldredge, Hodder & Stoughton, 2013.

They Shall Expel Demons: What You Need to Know About Demons – Your Invisible Enemies
Derek Prince, DPM, 1998.

Trapped by Control: How to Find Freedom
David Cross, Sovereign World, 2008.

Victory Over Darkness: Realize the Power of Your Identity in Christ
Dr Neil T. Anderson, Regal, 1990.

ABOUT THE AUTHOR

David Legge lives in Portadown, Northern Ireland, with his wife, Barbara, and their children, Lydia and Noah. David was involved in pastoral ministry for eleven years, before embarking upon an itinerant preaching ministry in 2008. He spends much of his time ministering personally to people in prayer, both at the meetings he takes and in his own home. His preaching ministry is available online at *preachtheword.com*.